Puzzles to Challenge Your Mind

Consultant: Elkhonon Goldberg, Ph.D.

Publications International, Ltd.

Elkhonon Goldberg, Ph.D., ABPP/ABCN (consultant) is a clinical professor of neurology at New York University School of Medicine, a diplomate of the American Board of Professional Psychology/American Board of Clinical Neuropsychology, and director of The East-West Science and Education Foundation. Dr. Goldberg created the Manhattan-based Cognitive Enhancement Program, a fitness center for the brain, and is author of the international best-selling books *The Wisdom Paradox: How Your Mind Can Grow as Your Brain Grows Older* and *The Executive Brain: Frontal Lobes and the Civilized Mind.*

Julie K. Cohen is a puzzle developer, puzzle consultant, author, and freelance writer. She has published numerous math puzzle books, and her puzzles for children and adults appear in national magazines, Web sites, puzzle books, cellular phone games, and DVDs. To learn more about Cohen, visit her Web site, http://www.JulieKCohen.com.

Amy Reynaldo, the author of *How to Conquer the New York Times Crossword Puzzle,* created the first crossword blog (Diary of a Crossword Fiend) and reviews 1,500 crosswords a year. She is a top-10 finisher at the American Crossword Puzzle Tournament.

Puzzle Constructors: Michael Adams, Cihan Altay, Myles Callum, Philip Carter, Kelly Clark, Barry Clarke, Conceptis Puzzles, Don Cook, Jeanette Dall, Mark Danna, Harvey Estes, Josie Faulkner, Adrian Fisher, Connie Formby, Erich Friedman, Serhiy Grabarchuk, Ray Hamel, Luke Haward, Marilynn Huret, Kate Mepham, Patrick Merrell, David Millar, Dan Moore, Michael Moreci, Elsa Neal, Alan Olschwang, Stephen Ryder, Gianni Sarcone, Pete Sarjeant, Paul Seaburn, Fraser Simpson, Terry Stickels, Howard Tomlinson. Wayne Robert Williams

Illustrators: Hyelim An, Elizabeth Gerber, Nicole H. Lee, Jay Sato, Shavan R. Spears, Jen Torche

Louis Weber, CEO
Publications International, Ltd.
7373 North Cicero Avenue
Lincolnwood, Illinois 60712

Permission is never granted for commercial purposes.

ISBN-13: 978-1-60553-342-1
ISBN-10: 1-60553-342-4

Manufactured in China.

8 7 6 5 4 3 2 1

Contents

A Cognitive Workout

The fountain of youth exists only in folklore and fairy tales, but that hasn't stopped professionals, laypeople, and everyone in between from attempting to uncover the secrets behind good health and longevity. We all want to stay young and active in order to lead fulfilling lives, but to achieve this, we have to keep our bodies *and* our minds in top shape. How do we do this? Well, there is plenty of information regarding the care of our bodies, but relatively little attention has been paid to the importance of taking care of our minds. That's why this publication is so valuable. *Brain Games™: Puzzles to Challenge Your Mind* is an excellent resource that will help you keep your brain fit for life.

The human brain thrives on learning and experiencing new things—it is stimulated by both novelty and challenge. If something is routine or too easy, our brains are essentially operating on autopilot—which doesn't require a lot of mental attention and does little to boost cerebral strength. By exposing ourselves to new activities and information, we are exercising our brains in a way that will keep them sharp and focused.

To maintain cognitive fitness, you have to get your head in the game (pun intended). "Use it or lose it!" should be your motto from now on, and working the puzzles in this publication is a great way to put those words into action so you can start to benefit from them.

Researchers use the term "cognitive reserve" to explain the importance of building brain power from an early age. In doing so, you are creating a "cushion" that will keep your brain in good

operating order as you get older. But it's never too late to start working on brain fitness. "Now" is the best time to learn to play a musical instrument, to enroll in a new class—and to take advantage of all this publication has to offer.

Take a few minutes to familiarize yourself with the wide variety of puzzles in this book (as well as their levels of difficulty). Different kinds of puzzles stimulate different parts of the brain, and you should exercise as many of those areas as possible. To help you choose the puzzles that will provide the most benefit, we've labeled each one with the cognitive functions it exercises (computation, language, logic, and memory are just a few). Consider doing a variety of puzzles each day so that you don't limit the scope of your workout. Like physical fitness, cognitive fitness can be the result of consistently challenging—and varied—workouts.

Finally, don't forget that puzzles are a lot of fun to solve—think of the simple enjoyment you derive from working a crossword or finding your way through a twisting maze. The pleasure of sitting back and doing a puzzle is not only relaxing—it can also help relieve stress after a long day. Another great thing about this publication is that it's

small enough to carry anywhere: to the park, the doctor's office, or on a trip out of town. Whenever you have a chance, turn your downtime into brain-boosting time—and think of the fun you'll have while doing it!

Warm Up Your Brain

Quic-Kross

LANGUAGE

GENERAL KNOWLEDGE

This is a crossword puzzle with a twist. Use the clues to solve the puzzle. When complete, the circled letters will spell out a "mystery word."

Across

1. Chest bone

2. Have (past tense)

3. Offer

Down

4. It is (abb.)

5. Venomous reptile

6. Burnt wood residue

Mystery word clue: Vegetable

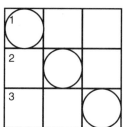

Anagrams at Work

LANGUAGE

Fill in the blanks in the sentence below with 7-letter words that are anagrams (rearrangements of the same letters) of one another.

The 4-star _____ asked his assistant to

_____ the photograph so he could get

a closer view of the intended target.

Answers on page 171.

Crossed Words

Write each word below in the grid. They will fit only one way.

3 Letters
CAR
CAT

4 Letters
BABY
BELL
BOAT
FISH

PLAY
ROSE
SHOE
SNOW

5 Letters
HORSE
HOUSE

6 Letters
FARMER
FATHER
FLOWER
MOTHER

8 Letters
AIRPLANE

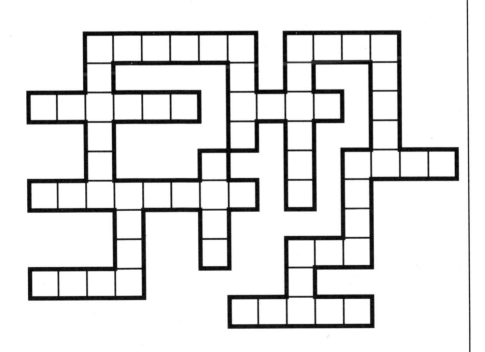

1-2-3

Place the numbers 1, 2, or 3 in the circles below. The challenge is to have only these 3 numbers in each connected row and column—no number should repeat. Any combination is allowed.

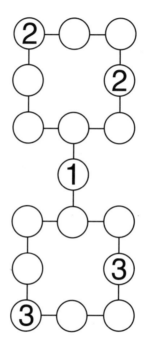

 Trivia on the Brain

Studies have noted that over the last few centuries, there's an increase in average brain size of about 0.5 percent per decade.

Answer on page 171.

Odd One Out

Can you determine which of the words below is the odd one out?

Hint: Think about sounds and meanings.

I   HE   HEAL   KNOWS

ANALYSIS LOGIC

L'adder

Starting at the bottom rung, use the numbers 1 through 9 to add up to the top number. Numbers can only be used once. There's a catch though: The precise sums must be met along the way.

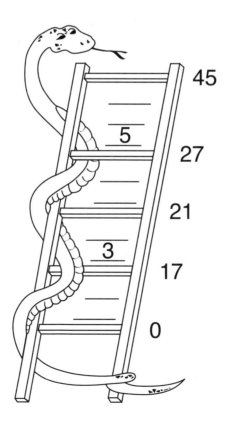

45

___

5

27

___

21

___

3

17

___

0

ANALYSIS COMPUTATION

Perfect Score

Make 3 successful hits so that the sum of the numbers is 100. Double and triple scores do not apply. Numbers may be used more than once.

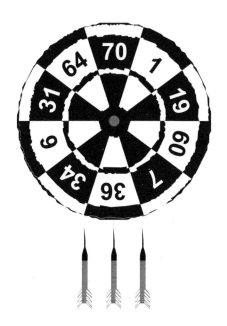

Trivia on the Brain

We dream about 4 or 5 times a night, so people reaching 80 years old will have had approximately 131,400 dreams in their lifetimes. How many dreams have you had, and how many can you remember?

Answer on page 171.

Sudoku

Use deductive logic to complete the grid so that each row, each column, and each 3 by 3 box contains the numbers 1 through 9 in some order. The solution is unique.

2					7		4	5
		5	2			7	1	
		6	5				2	9
			6					4
5	1	4	3		9	2	6	7
9					2			
6	4				1	5		
	5	2			4	1		
3	8		7					2

Three of a Kind

Fill in the blanks in the sentences below with 3-letter words that are anagrams (rearrangements of the same letters) of one another.

1. Dad hurt his _____ when the big _____ knocked him into the fence.

2. The Queen said, "I _____ thee Sir _____."

3. I felt a little _____ when the _____ stuck my finger.

4. My pet _____ didn't _____ normally.

5. The wall looked _____ with the _____ of dirt on it.

Answers on page 171. **11**

Marbles

Place 8 marbles into the grid without having any touch one another, not even diagonally. There are some walls, represented by thick lines, that block the view of the marbles. Marbles must not "see" each other in a horizontal or vertical direction. We've placed 1 to get you started.

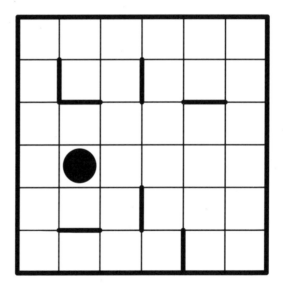

Answer on page 171.

Hashi

Each circle represents an island, with the number inside indicating the number of bridges connected to it. Draw bridges between islands using the number given. There can be no more than 2 bridges going in the same direction, and there must be a continuous path connecting all islands. Bridges can only be vertical or horizontal and may not cross islands or other bridges. We've drawn some bridges to get you started.

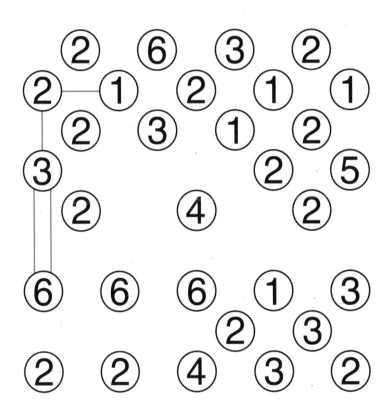

Cross Count

All the letters of the alphabet have been assigned a value from 1 through 9, as demonstrated in the box below. Fill in the grid with common English words so that the rows and columns add up correctly.

1	2	3	4	5	6	7	8	9
a	b	c	d	e	f	g	h	i
j	k	l	m	n	o	p	q	r
s	t	u	v	w	x	y	z	

	8	5	14
		5	17
a			10
9	18	14	

Trivia on the Brain

Your brain allows you to differentiate between 3,000 and 10,000 distinct smells. Who "nose" if you'd be able to smell anything at all without it!

Answer on page 172.

Number Climber

Help the mountaineer reach the summit by filling the boulder circles with numbers. Each boulder is the sum of the 2 numbers in the boulder that support it. For example: 2 + 3 = 5. If a total is 10 or more, only write in the second digit. For example: 7 + 6 = 13; write in 3.

Job Jibes

True to his name, our pal Josh has defined 8 jobs in a joshing way. Can you use his humorous definition to place the job titles in the freeform crossword on the next page? When you figure out one answer, its letters may help you solve other clues.

Across

   1. One who thinks change is inevitable?

   3. One who really digs their job?

   7. One who has lots of promise?

   8. One who has class?

Down

   2. One who is patently smart?

   4. One who's home on the range?

   5. One with novel ideas?

   6. One who is outstanding in his field?

ARCHAEOLOGIST	COOK
INVENTOR	REALTOR
CASHIER	FARMER
LIBRARIAN	TEACHER

⚙ Trivia on the Brain

The world's largest crossword puzzle is seven feet high and seven feet wide. There are more than 28,000 unique clues and 91,000 boxes. Want to give it a try? A copy of this crossword is available for purchase at various retail establishments.

Army Show

The army entertainment troupe members have determined the order in which their acts will go on stage, but the stage manager has mixed up the order on his list. Although each item is in the correct column, only one item in each column is correctly positioned. The following facts are true about the correct order:

1. Private is not second.

2. Acting is 1 place below Bark.

3. Buckshot is not second.

4. Buckshot is 1 place above Major.

5. Colonel is 1 place below comedy.

6. Rattle is third.

Can you determine the title, surname, and act for each position?

	Title	Surname	Act
1	Private	Buckshot	comedy
2	Colonel	Trumpet	piano
3	Sergeant	Bark	acting
4	Major	Rattle	juggling

Answers on page 172.

Contain Yourself

For the clues below, look for a small word that fits in a larger "container" word. For example, "vegetable in a weapon (3 letters in 5 letters)" would be s(pea)r.

Writing implement in a description of price (3 letters in 9 letters)

_____

Satanic character in old-style theatrical entertainment (5 letters in 10 letters) _____

"Messiah" composer in overhead light fixture (6 letters in 10 letters) _____

You Can Count on This

Cryptograms are messages in substitution code. Break the code to read the humorous observation. For example, THE SMART CAT might become FVO QWGDF JGF if **F** is substituted for **T**, **V** for **H**, **O** for **E**, and so on.

LN CAU GTDB AXB HXZCUB MY CT

MYU CAU FUCDLE YWYCUF, CAUDU

HTMGB AXJU VUUZ CUZ XITYCGUY.

The Shading Game

Use a pencil or highlighter to shade all of the squares that contain the numeral 3. The shaded area will spell out the answer to this riddle: What did the baseball player do when he couldn't hit right?

4	5	1	9	8	2	4	1	0	8	7	6	0	7	4
7	6	3	4	3	8	7	3	1	9	3	3	3	7	8
2	9	3	1	3	5	5	3	6	7	5	3	9	8	1
8	4	3	3	3	7	8	3	4	5	2	3	2	2	9
6	4	3	5	3	4	9	3	6	0	7	3	2	7	8
7	9	3	4	3	7	7	3	2	0	4	3	1	5	6
5	0	9	1	4	2	7	6	8	7	1	9	4	6	4
6	4	5	8	7	1	2	2	9	9	0	7	1	5	7
3	5	6	2	3	3	3	9	3	3	3	7	3	3	3
3	7	6	9	3	5	6	2	3	7	6	9	8	3	4
3	4	1	7	3	3	8	7	3	3	2	1	5	3	4
3	9	8	5	3	2	4	1	3	6	5	7	9	3	0
3	3	3	6	3	3	3	1	3	4	5	9	2	3	7
5	6	5	9	8	1	2	0	4	6	5	8	1	9	7
6	6	9	1	8	2	4	2	2	0	9	8	1	7	5

Answer on page 172.

Word Columns

Find the hidden humorous statement by using the letters directly below each of the blank squares. Each letter is used only once. A black square indicates the end of a word.

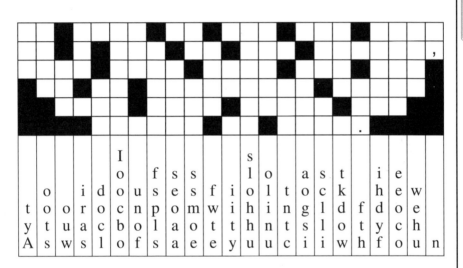

					I							s											
					o		f	s	s			l	o		a			t		i	e		
	o		i	d	o	u	s	e	s	f	i	o	l	t	o	c	k			h	e	w	
t	o	o	r	o	c	n	p	o	m	w	i	h	i	n	g	l	d	f		d	o	e	
y	t	u	a	c	b	o	l	a	o	t	t	h	n	t	s	l	o	t	y	y	c	h	
A	s	w	s	l	o	f	s	e	a	e	y	u	u	c	i	i	w	h	f	o	u	n	n

Trivia on the Brain

Ever have trouble remembering something that you know ought to be easy to recall? Turns out your brain has to forget things to make room for new memories. Now if only your brain could remember where you put your car keys instead of what you ate for breakfast this morning!

Between the Lines

Solve for the middle (undefined) words in each set. For each group, all 3 words appear on the same page in the dictionary in the order they are given. By figuring out what the first and third words are, you should be able to identify the middle word. Rearrange the middle words from each set to complete the quote on the next page.

Example:

a) putter: to work at random; tinker

b) puzzle

c) pygmy: one of a race of dwarfs

a) _ _ m m _ _ _ : any of numerous extinct Pleistocene elephants

b) _ _ _

c) _ _ _ _ _ l _ : a shackle for the hand or wrist

a) _ _ m p u _ : a usually noisy commotion

b) r _ _

c) _ _ _ a _ _ _ : a fugitive

a) _ _ _ _ _ _ _ _ p t : a document written by hand or typed, as
                               opposed to printed

b) _ _ n y

c) _ _ p : a representation of an area of land or sea

a) _ _ s _ _ : the upright member between two stair treads

b) _ _ s _

c) _ _ _ q _ _ : verging on impropriety or indecency

a) _ _ s t _ _ : a female having the same parents as another person

b) _ i _

c) _ _ _ a _ : an Indian lute

"A _____ _____(s) as _____ _____(s)
as he _____ ."

—Henry David Thoreau

Word Jigsaw

Fit the pieces into the frame to form common, uncapitalized words reading across and down. There's no need to rotate the pieces; they'll fit as shown, with each piece used exactly once.

The Fruit Vendor's Cart

Help a fruit vendor with an overturned cart gather all the fruit and put it back on his cart. The list below shows each kind of fruit he had on his cart. The grid represents the only way the cart can be organized to hold all the fruit. Put each word in place so the vendor can get on his way.

APPLE

APRICOT

AVOCADO

BANANA

CHERRY

FIG

GRAPE

LEMON

LIME

ORANGE

PEACH

PEAR

STRAWBERRY

TANGERINE

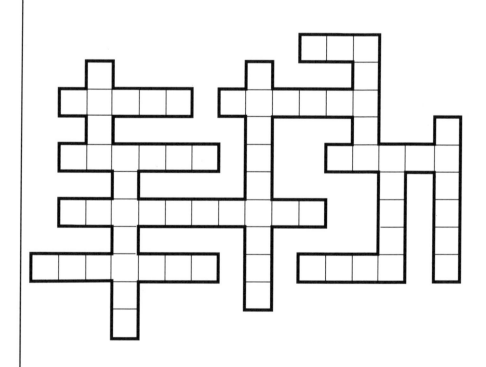

Answers on page 173.

Fences

Connect the dots and draw a continuous path that doesn't cross itself. Numbers represent the "fences" created by the path (2 edges are created around the number 2, 3 edges around 3, etc.). We've started the puzzle for you.

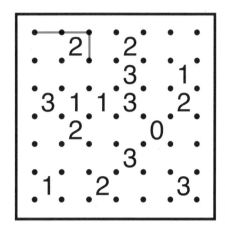

Word Ladder

Use the clues to change just 1 letter on each line to go from the top word to the bottom word. Do not change the order of the letters. You must have a common English word at each step.

BLOND

_____ tasteless

_____ to stamp with ownership

BRAID

Honeycomb

There are 16 letters in the honeycomb below that are surrounded by different letters (no letters are repeated). Can you find them all?

☼ Trivia on the Brain

The Dole Food Company has created the world's largest permanent hedge maze in Hawaii. If you're not careful, you might get lost in the 2.46 miles of paths that make up the maze.

Answer on page 173.

Code-doku

Solve this puzzle just as you would a sudoku. Use deductive logic to complete the grid so that each row, each column, and each 3 by 3 box contains each of the letters AEGHIMNWY in some order. The solution is unique.

When you have completed the puzzle, unscramble those 9 letters to reveal the name of a modernist writer known for his love of bullfighting.

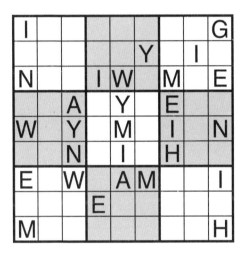

Answer: _____

Odd One Out

Can you determine which of the words below is the odd one out?

Hint: Think about meanings.

BEAR   SOW   DUCK   HEN

Hashi

Each circle represents an island, with the number inside
indicating the number of bridges connected to it. Draw bridges
between islands using the number given. There can be no more
than 2 bridges going in the same direction, and there must be
a continuous path connecting all islands. Bridges can only be
vertical or horizontal and may not cross islands or other bridges.
We've drawn some bridges to get you started.

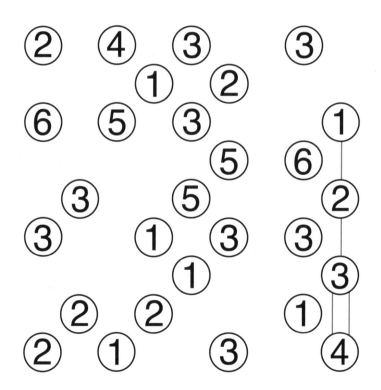

Answer on page 173.

Flying High

Unscramble the names of these common birds and write their names in the boxes provided. Then place the letters in the numbered squares into the corresponding boxes below to reveal a phrase related to the theme of this puzzle.

COANFL	1							
RIOBN			8					
CAALINRD		7		11				
NAARYC					10			
BIRDULEB				4				
WOCR		2						
EGLAE					3			
WSROPRA			5					
GASLIRNT	6					9		

1 2 3 4   5 6   7   8 9 10 11

Answer on page 173.

On the Slant

Solve the crossword clues to fill in this 5 by 5 grid. When you are finished, the shaded diagonal squares will spell out a word.

Across

1. Mower's cut

6. "Shucks!"

7. Approaches

8. Holds tight to

9. Detect

Down

1. "That's Amore" and others

2. What treasure hunters want to know

3. One more time

4. Maryland players

5. Steppenwolf author

1	2	3	4	5
6				
7				
8				
9				

Diagonal word: _____

Answers on page 174.

A Puzzling Perspective

Mentally arrange the lettered balls from large to small in the correct order to spell an 11-letter word.

Clue: Senior year events

Trivia on the Brain

Famous names are popular words for making anagrams. For example, within "Florence Nightingale" you can find "flit on, cheering angel," and within "Clint Eastwood" you'll find "old west action."

ANALYSIS

Name Calling

Decipher the encoded words in the proverb below using the numbers and letters on the phone pad. Remember that each number can stand for 3 or 4 possible letters.

2–2–7–8 in your lot 2–6–6–6–4 us, let us all have one 7–8–7–7–3.

CREATIVE THINKING

ANALYSIS

A Beatles' Triple Sequence

Can you complete this sequence?

A T M ___

32

Number Crossword

Fill in this crossword with numbers instead of letters. Use the clues to determine which number from 1 through 8 belongs in each empty square. No zeros are used.

1	2	3	
4			5
6			
	7		

Across

1. Consecutive even digits

4. Consecutive digits, ascending

6. Each of its digits (after the first one) is double the previous digit

7. A multiple of 59

Down

1. Consecutive digits out of order

2. A number in the form of AABB

3. Consecutive digits, descending

5. A palindrome

Acrostic Clues

Solve the clues below, and then place the letters in their corresponding spots in the grid on the next page to reveal an inspirational quote. The letter in the upper-right corner of each grid square refers to the clue the letter comes from.

A. Author of quote (3 words)

$\overline{32}$ $\overline{22}$ $\overline{5}$ $\overline{53}$ $\overline{61}$ $\overline{68}$ $\overline{54}$ $\overline{64}$ $\overline{57}$ $\overline{59}$

$\overline{7}$ $\overline{43}$ $\overline{10}$ $\overline{37}$ $\overline{35}$ $\overline{31}$ $\overline{73}$

B. Largest country

$\overline{55}$ $\overline{15}$ $\overline{49}$ $\overline{8}$ $\overline{72}$ $\overline{17}$

C. Nobel's invention

$\overline{14}$ $\overline{42}$ $\overline{18}$ $\overline{62}$ $\overline{52}$ $\overline{65}$ $\overline{45}$ $\overline{38}$

D. Dud or failure

$\overline{20}$ $\overline{44}$ $\overline{67}$ $\overline{2}$ $\overline{51}$ $\overline{74}$ $\overline{63}$

E. Takes the stand

$\overline{46}$ $\overline{29}$ $\overline{75}$ $\overline{58}$ $\overline{12}$ $\overline{30}$ $\overline{25}$ $\overline{47}$ $\overline{27}$

F. Scandinavian country

$\overline{16}$ $\overline{1}$ $\overline{26}$ $\overline{19}$ $\overline{66}$ $\overline{41}$

G. Sleep through winter

— — — — — — — — —
71 6 9 33 48 13 3 70 56

H. Large flatfish

— — — — — — —
21 36 24 40 28 34 39

I. Jerk

— — — — — —
23 60 69 4 50 11

1 F	2 D	3 G	4 I		5 A	6 G	7 A	8 B		9 G	10 A	11 I	12 E	13 G	14 C		15 B
17 B	18 C	19 F		20 D	21 H	22 A	23 I		24 H	25 E	26 F	27 E		28 H	29 E	30 E	31 A
	34 H	35 A		36 H	37 A	38 C		39 H	40 H	41 F	42 C		43 A	44 D	45 C	46 E	47 E
	50 I	51 D	52 C	53 A	54 A	55 B	56 G	57 A		58 E	59 A		60 I	61 A	62 C	63 D	
64 A	65 C	66 F	67 D		68 A	69 I	70 G	71 G	72 B	73 A		74 D	75 E				

Trivia on the Brain

Palindromes are words or phrases that are spelled the same backward and forward, such as "Mom" or "race car." Though no one is really afraid of palindromes, the phobia of them has been humorously called "aibohphobia," which—of course—is a palindrome in itself!

Cone You Top This?

In the mood for summer weather, picnics, and the ice-cream truck? This word search is just the thing! Every word listed below is contained within the group of letters on the next page. The words can be found in a straight line horizontally, vertically, or diagonally. The words may read either backward or forward.

BARBECUE

BASEBALL

BOATING

BURN

CAMPFIRE

CAMPING

CANOEING

DAYLIGHT

DIVING

GARDEN

GRILL

HAMBURGERS

HAMMOCK

HEAT

HIKING

HOME

HOT DOGS

ICE CREAM

JET SKI

KAYAKING

LEISURE

MOTOR

MOW

OUTDOORS

PARK

PICNIC

PLAYGROUND

POOL

POPSICLE

RAFTING

SAILING

SIGHTSEEING

SNOW CONE

SPRINKLER

SUN

SWIMMING

SWING

TAN

TENT

TRAILER

TRIP

TUBING

WATERSKIING

WORK

VACATION

YARD

```
        V T E N T O I G
      A K X R Z U W P A D G L
    X N A T A E S G L Z A A B T
  P G O Y D I R N E A K Y R U S U
  U N I A T L I O O Y K L D R Y D
  G I T K J E F W B G S I E N O M
P N P A I O R P C B R P G N I V I D
O I M C N E M M O T O R H O M E E T
O B A A G L O A N U U I T Z G R K H
A L U C V Y C T C E B N N Z R U R A T O
  T T T L I A W M R D K I S O M P
  B B D N S E A O R C L I W M I P
  S G G O P H T W P L E D O C G P
    W N A O A E I Q L R C N N L
    I I P R R N O A K I I B
      N M T S K Y B C E T
      G M K C J E E U
      N X I G E S G C
      I K I W T A N E
      L L N H S B I B
      I S G B K Y K R
      A I M J I N I A
      S G O D T O H B
      G N I T F A R B
      J E P N V M R B
```

LEVEL 2 Get Your Mind Moving
Vowel Play

In the freeform crossword on the next page, each word or phrase contains the vowels **A, E, I, O,** and **U,** though not necessarily in that order. When you figure out one answer, its letters may help you solve other clues.

Across

2. Holding fast; persistent

5. Entree

7. Giant tree of California

9. State of extreme fatigue

10. Limits

Down

1. French farewell

3. Warned

4. Playground challenge

6. Broccoli relative

8. Jesting; not meant to be taken seriously

Match-Up Twins

The 10 hexagons below may look identical at first glance, but they're not. They can actually be divided into 5 pairs of identical designs. Can you match them up?

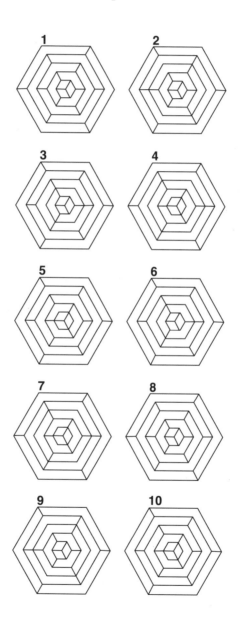

Answers on page 174.

Word of Mouth

Solve this puzzle just as you would a sudoku. Use deductive logic to complete the grid so that each row, each column, and each long diagonal contains each of the letters of the word MOUTH in some order. The solution is unique. We've inserted 6 letters to get you started.

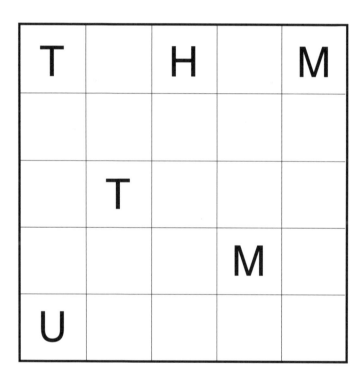

Hashi

Each circle represents an island, with the number inside indicating the number of bridges connected to it. Draw bridges between islands using the number given. There can be no more than 2 bridges going in the same direction, and there must be a continuous path connecting all islands. Bridges can only be vertical or horizontal and may not cross islands or other bridges. We've drawn some bridges to get you started.

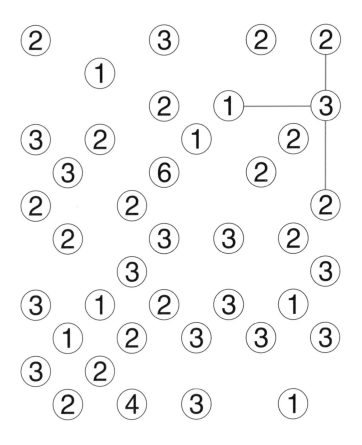

Answer on page 175.

Elevator Words

Like an elevator, words move up and down the "floors" of this puzzle. Starting with the first answer, the second word from each answer carries down to become the first word of the following answer. With the clues given, complete the puzzle.

1. Know _____

2. _____ _____

3. _____ _____

4. _____ _____

5. _____ _____

6. _____ _____

7. _____ Hit

Clues

1. Expertise
2. "Why?"
3. Confess
4. Innocence

5. "Don't Touch!"
6. Mistaken
7. Single, in baseball

Missing Connections

It's a crossword without the clues! Use the letters below to fill in the empty spaces in the crossword grid. When you are finished, you'll have words that read both across and down, crossword-style.

A A A A B C D D E E E H L M

M M O P P P R R R R S S T T T T T T Y

Answers on page 175.

Geometric Cube Construction

ANALYSIS
LOGIC

Which one of the cubes can be made from the unfolded sample?

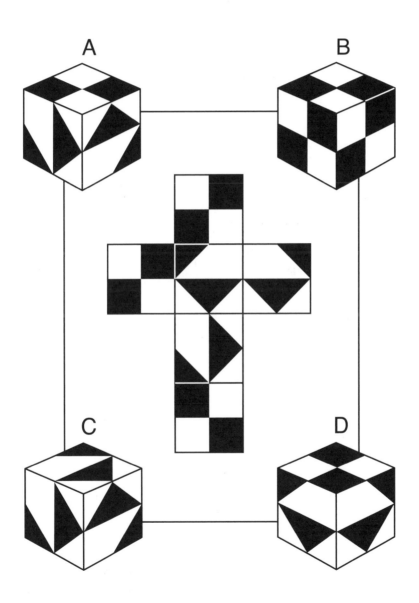

Star Power

Fill in each empty square in the grid so that each star is surrounded by the numbers 1 through 8 with no repeats.

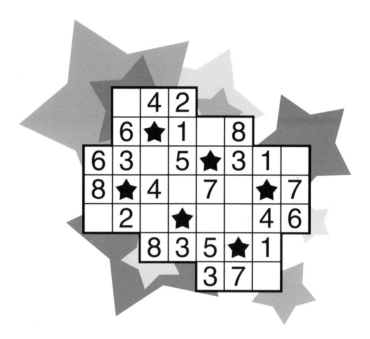

Trivia on the Brain

The brain continues to generate new neurons throughout nearly all its life—even into its seventies!

Answer on page 175.

Kakuro

Place a number from 1 through 9 in each empty cell so that the sum of each vertical or horizontal run (rows and columns extending from already numbered cells) equals the number at the top or on the left of that run. Numbers may not be repeated in any run, and runs end at dark-colored squares.

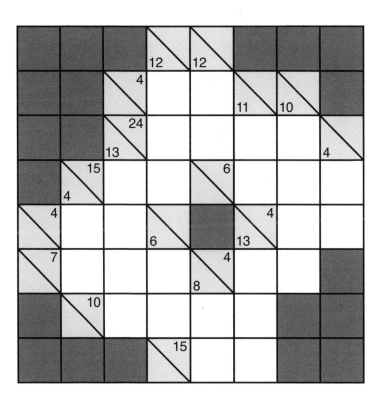

LANGUAGE

COMPUTATION

Cross Count

All the letters of the alphabet have been assigned a value from 1 through 9, as demonstrated in the box below. Fill in the grid with common English words so that the rows and columns add up correctly.

1	2	3	4	5	6	7	8	9
a	b	c	d	e	f	g	h	i
j	k	l	m	n	o	p	q	r
s	t	u	v	w	x	y	z	

⁹r			⁵	27
	b		⁵	11
	⁶	¹a		16
	⁵	⁵	s	13
18	19	16	14	

Answer on page 175.

Anagram Pickup

Fill in the blanks in the sentence below with 8-letter words that are anagrams (rearrangements of the same letters) of one another.

The handsome guy at the bar felt that he had been

_____ when the girl he'd been chatting up

wouldn't give him her _____ phone number.

Letters to Numbers

Each letter represents a number from 1 through 9. Use the clues to help you put the numbers in their places within the grid.

Clues:

1. G × G = F + H
2. B × G × J = A
3. B × D = D
4. D + D = G + J
5. E + H = B + C + F

A	B	C
D	E	F
G	H	J

Hint: Since D + D = G + J, G + J must be an even number.

Quic-Kross

This is a crossword puzzle with a twist. Use the clues to solve the puzzle. When complete, the circled letters will spell out a "mystery word."

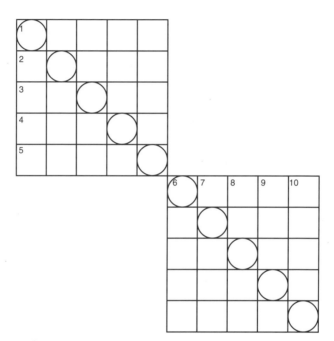

Across

1. Discuss heatedly

2. Small bay on ocean

3. Following

4. At front

5. Afterward

Down

6. Crunchy

7. Rock

8. Allotted time

9. Sofa

10. Spaghetti, for example

Mystery word clue: Continent

Answers on page 176.

Cube Count

How many individual cubes are in this configuration? Assume all rows and columns are complete unless you actually see them end.

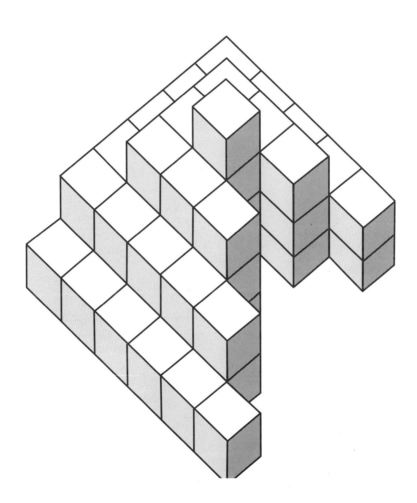

Crossing Caution

Across
1. Bovine baby
5. Shankar of sitar
9. Synagogue official
14. Cain's brother
15. Seuss's "If ____ the Zoo"
16. Kept in the dark
17. Fish in a melt
18. Unsteady gait
19. City near Florence
20. Breaking news order
23. Protrudes
24. Vine-covered
25. Sporty Chevy
28. Sneaker brand
29. New Deal prog.
32. Big name in gas
33. Furnace output
34. Restaurateur Toots
35. "You're one to spout off!"
38. Lodging providers
39. Skin moisturizer
40. Perform better than
41. NFL 3-pointers
42. Type of school
43. Annoy forcefully
44. Caribbean republic
46. Challenging chore
47. "Think it over"
52. Titanic-seeker's tool
53. Cry of frustration

54. Boat follower
55. Office worker
56. Cold war defense assn.
57. Former blade brand
58. Soda insert
59. Kind of jacket
60. Wine list datum

Down
1. Rodent exterminators
2. Share a border
3. Jay of TV
4. Pancakes
5. "Sure thing!"
6. Ovine sign
7. Theda Bara role
8. Behind closed doors
9. Putin's land
10. Liqueur flavoring
11. Use all the resources of
12. Waste containers
13. "Give _____ rest"
21. Novelist Scott
22. Madonna musical
25. Ariz. neighbor
26. In the midst of
27. White lightning maker
28. Noted fabulist
30. Polliwogs' places
31. Job-specific vocabulary
33. Golfer's dream

34. Leave stealthily
36. Author Bret
37. At large
42. NASCAR service area
43. Strand on an island
45. Yoga posture
46. Jay Silverheels role

47. Senator Trent
48. What this isn't
49. Glut
50. Gumbo vegetable
51. Get closer to
52. Draft letters

Word Jigsaw

Fit the pieces into the frame to form common words reading across and down. There's no need to rotate the pieces; they'll fit as shown, with each piece used exactly once.

Bonus: One of the nine words spelled will be the name of a character from the Bible.

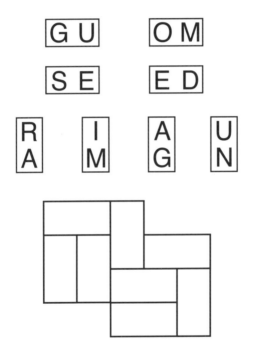

Trivia on the Brain

Your brain accounts for only about 2 percent of your body weight, but it uses more than 20 percent of your body's oxygen supply.

Answer on page 176.

Talk Show

On *The Jock Letterbox Show*, the producer has written down the guest list incorrectly. Although each entry is in the correct column only one entry in each column is correctly positioned. The following facts are true about the correct order:

1. Ponds is 1 place below book.

2. Bruce is 1 place above movie.

3. The discussion of a movie is not second.

4. Hal is 1 place above Wells.

Can you give the guest's name, surname, and topic for each position?

	Name	Surname	Topic
1	Hal	Bore	politics
2	Jackie	Rawlings	book
3	Bruce	Wells	movie
4	Gary	Ponds	baseball

Cluster

Fill in each grape so the number in descending rows is the total of the neighboring numbers from the row above it. Each grape contains a positive whole number. Numbers can be repeated.

Answer on page 176.

Dubious Dictionary

We're sure you enjoy reading the dictionary in your spare time—don't we all? But you probably won't find these definitions in your lexicon. We've entered a few letters in this freeform crossword to help you get started. When you figure out one answer, its letters may help you solve other clues.

Across
2. Trampoline artist?
3. Sidewalk engineer?
5. Body shop worker?
6. Clumsy ophthalmologist?

Down
1. Thinking about a hero?
4. One who can't keep a secret?

Word Columns

Find the hidden humorous statement by using the letters directly below each of the blank squares. Each letter is used only once. A black square indicates the end of a word.

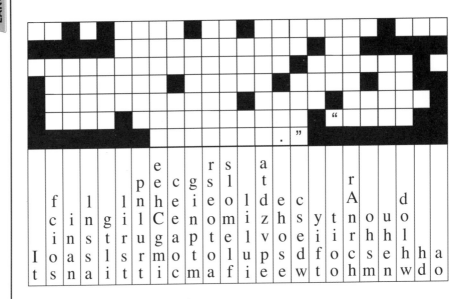

Trivia on the Brain

The weight of the human brain triples during the first year of life, going from about 300 grams to about 900 grams.

Answer on page 176.

Calcu-doku

Use arithmetic and deductive logic to complete the grid so that each row and each column contains the numbers 1 through 5 in some order. Numbers in each outlined set of squares combine to produce the number in the top corner using the mathematical sign indicated. The solution is unique.

8+			6×	4
1-	15×			6+
	2	5+		
7+	7+		7+	
		2/		3

Circle Takes the Square

All you have to do to solve this puzzle is move in a single unbroken path from the circle in the upper left corner to the circle in the lower right. Your path must alternate between circles and squares, and you can only move horizontally and vertically (not diagonally). There's only one way to do it.

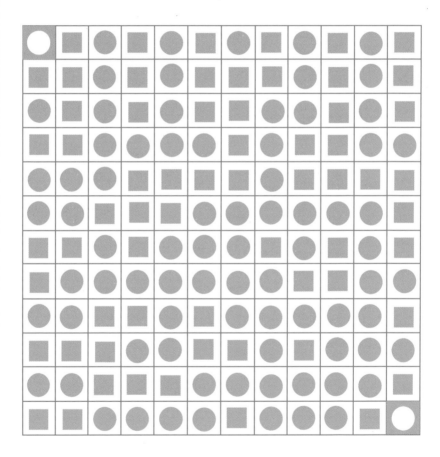

Answer on page 177.

Card Shark

All 13 cards in a single suit have been lined up in the row below. No two cards are in order. Can you discover which card is which using the clues given?

One court card is the last card on the right.

The 8 is one place to the right of the king and two places to the left of the queen.

From the left, the first and second cards equal 11; from the right, the second and third cards also equal 11.

The sixth card from the left is even, as is the third card from the right.

The ace is two places right of the 9, and three places left of the king.

The 3 is somewhere left of 6, which is left of 5; none are adjacent.

The jack is two places right of the 4.

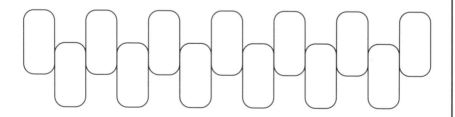

LOGIC
ANALYSIS

Marbles

Place 8 marbles into the grid without having any touch one another, not even diagonally. There are some walls, represented by thick lines, that block the view of the marbles. Marbles must not "see" each other in a horizontal or vertical direction. We've placed 1 to get you started.

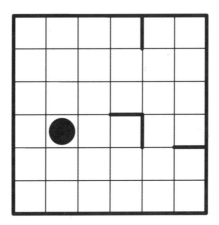

COMPUTATION
ANALYSIS

Take Me Out to the Ball Game

For millions of fans, baseball means the Yankees. Can you prove it true by substituting the letters below into numbers? Hint: Zero cannot begin a word. For this puzzle, A = 6, E = 8, K = 5, S = 4.

BASE

BALL

+ GAMES

———

YANKS

Answers on page 177.

Jewelry Scramblegram

LANGUAGE

Four 6-letter words, all of which revolve around the same theme, have been jumbled. Unscramble each word and write the answer in the accompanying space. Next, transfer the letters in the shaded boxes into the shaded keyword space, and unscramble the 8-letter word that goes with the theme. The theme for this puzzle is jewelry.

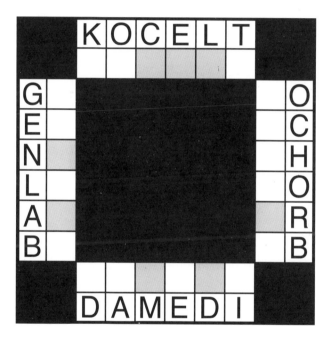

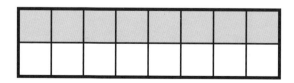

Sudoku

Use deductive logic to complete the grid so that each row, each column, and each 3 by 3 box contains the numbers 1 through 9 in some order. The solution is unique.

	1	9		7				6
	2					7	8	5
				2		9		
8			6		2		3	
	2		4		7		5	
	5		1		8			2
	3			6				
1	8	5				6		
9				8		2	4	

Answer on page 177.

L'adder

Starting at the bottom rung, use the numbers 1 through 9 to add up to the top number. Numbers can only be used once. There's a catch though: The precise sums must be met along the way.

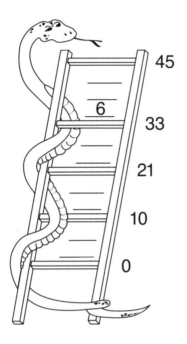

45

33

21

10

0

☼ Trivia on the Brain

Most people dream about 5 times every night, but we don't remember most dreams. We can only recall dreams that were interrupted.

Answer on page 177.

Number Challenge

Fill in the crossword on the next page with numbers instead of letters. Use the clues to determine which number from 1 through 9 belongs in each square. No zeros are used.

Across

1. A multiple of 7

3. A prime number

5. Consecutive digits, ascending

7. 10-Across plus 700

8. Five different odd numbers, out of order

10. 11-Across plus 10

11. A multiple of 5

Down

1. A multiple of 11

2. Five different odd numbers, out of order

3. A palindrome that is 8-Across minus 2-Down

4. The square of an even square

6. The first and last digits add up to the middle digit

8. A multiple of 11

9. A multiple of 5

1	2	■	3	4
5		6		
■	7			■
8				9
10		■	11	

Say What?

Below are a group of words that, when properly arranged in the blanks, reveal a quote from Thomas Edison.

pile   invent   you   a   good   junk   imagination

To _____, _____ need a _____ _____ and _____ _____ of _____.

1-2-3

Place the numbers 1, 2, or 3 in the circles below. The challenge is to have only these 3 numbers in each connected row and column—no number should repeat. Any combination is allowed.

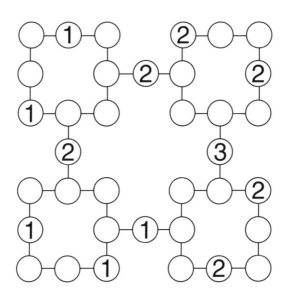

Trivia on the Brain

The brain contains as many neurons as there are stars in the Milky Way. The brain never "turns off" (or even rests) throughout your entire life!

Answer on page 178.

Name Search

Two friends had a contest to see who could hide their name more times in this grid. One of them won by only 1! Reading their 3-letter names forward, backward, up, down, and diagonally, can you figure out the winner?

Each of them has also hidden the same 3-letter spherical object word in the grid. Can you figure out what that word is?

Fitting Words

In this miniature crossword, the clues are listed randomly and are numbered for convenience only. It is up to you to figure out the placement of the 9 answers. To help you, we've inserted 1 letter in the grid, and this is the only occurrence of that letter in the puzzle.

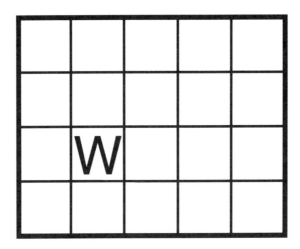

1. Fibber

2. Abraham's wife

3. Aplomb

4. Third son of Adam and Eve

5. Corn Belt state

6. Largest continent

7. Health resorts

8. Anticipate

9. He replaced Barnabas as Paul's traveling companion (Acts 15:40)

Answers on page 178.

LEVEL 3 Increase the Intensity
Odd-Even Logidoku

The numbers 1 through 9 are to appear once in every row, column, long diagonal, irregular shape, and 3 by 3 box. Cells marked with the letter **E** contain even numbers. From the numbers given, can you complete the puzzle?

Answer on page 178.

Warning: Curves Ahead

If you get lost, don't look at us—it wouldn't be the first time curves had led someone astray. You can travel under bridges.

START

FINISH

Answer on page 178.

ABCD

Every cell in this grid contains one of 4 letters: A, B, C, or D. No letter can be horizontally or vertically adjacent to itself. The tables above and to the left of the grid indicate how many times each letter appears in that column or row.

Can you complete the grid?

				A	2	1	2	2	2	0
				B	0	3	1	3	1	2
				C	2	2	2	0	1	1
A	B	C	D	2	0	1	1	2	3
3	2	0	1						
1	2	1	2						
0	2	3	1						
3	1	1	1						
0	2	3	1						
2	1	0	3						

Perfect Score

Make 3 successful hits so that the sum of the numbers is 100. Double and triple scores do not apply. Numbers may be used more than once.

☼ Trivia on the Brain

You know that time during the afternoon that you tend to feel sluggish? Turns out that's your brain telling you that you really need a nap. Studies have shown that a short nap (20 to 30 minutes) during this time can really boost your productivity.

Answer on page 178.

Star Power

Fill in each empty square in the grid so that each star is surrounded by the numbers 1 through 8 with no repeats.

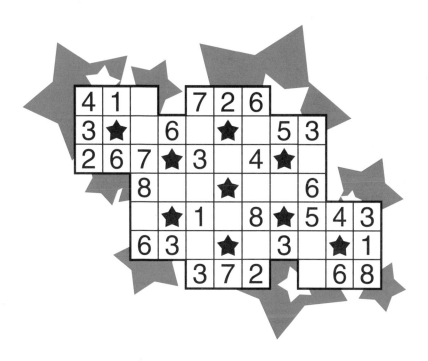

Spell Math!

Spell out numbers in the blanks below to obtain the correct solution. Numbers are used only once and range from 1 to 20. A letter has been given to get you started.

T __ __ + __ __ __ __ __ __ __ __ =

__ __ __ __ __ __

LOGIC

ANALYSIS

Card Shark

All 13 cards in a single suit have been lined up in the row below. No two cards are in order. Can you discover which card is which using the clues given?

No court cards are at either end.

Two court cards are adjacent; the king and the ace are separated by one card.

From the left, the second and third cards equal 13; the tenth and eleventh equal 10

The 8 is two places to the left of the ace.

The jack is two places the right of the 2.

The 4 is two places to the right of the 3.

The 6 is three places to the left of the ace.

The 9 is somewhere to the right of the 4.

The 10 is two places to the right of the 5.

The third card from the right is odd, as is the third card from the left.

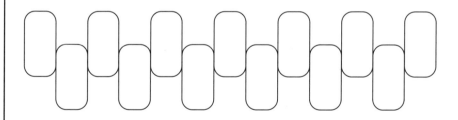

Answer on page 179.

Hashi

Each circle represents an island, with the number inside indicating the number of bridges connected to it. Draw bridges between islands using the number given. There can be no more than 2 bridges going in the same direction, and there must be a continuous path connecting all islands. Bridges can only be vertical or horizontal and may not cross islands or other bridges. We've drawn some bridges to get you started.

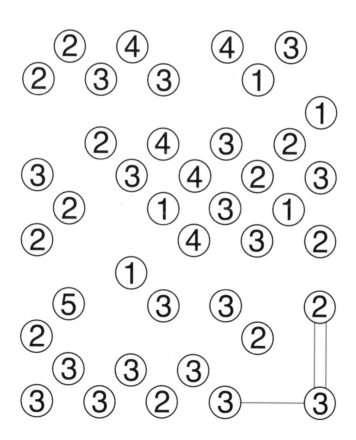

Wonders Down Under

In the freeform crossword on the next page, each word or phrase is associated with Australia. When you figure out one answer, its letters may help you solve the other clues.

Across

2. Throwing stick that returns

6. Smaller relative of the ostrich

8. Eucalyptus-eating marsupial

9. Egg-laying mammal of Australia and New Zealand

10. Large sandstone formation in Australia

Down

1. Type of eucalyptus that grows near billabongs

3. Everyday greeting Down Under

4. It's used for carrying food

5. Australian sheep

7. Word that means backwater or static lake

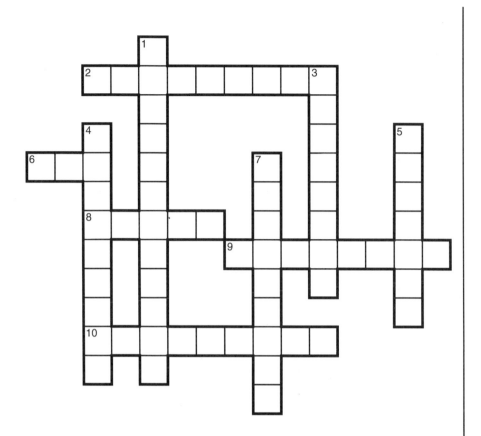

Trivia on the Brain

In the 1920s, crosswords became so popular that people began wearing clothing and jewelry that resembled the puzzle's distinctive motif.

Fashionable Scramblegram

Four 8-letter words, all of which revolve around the same theme, have been jumbled. Unscramble each word, and write the answer in the accompanying space. Next, transfer the letters in the shaded boxes into the shaded keyword space, and unscramble the 9-letter word that goes with the theme. The theme for this puzzle is clothing.

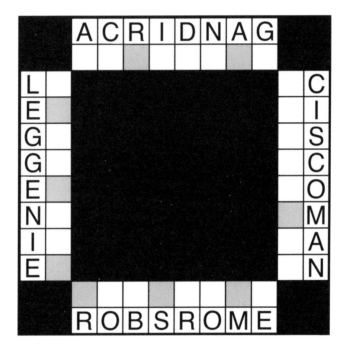

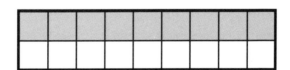

Answers on page 179.

Identity Parade

Oops! Four mugshots accidentally got sent through the shredder, and Officer Cuse is trying to straighten them out. Currently, only one facial feature in each row is in its correct place. Officer Cuse knows that:

1. C's eyes are 1 place to the left of his hair and 2 places to the right of D's nose.

2. A's mouth is 1 place to the left of B's eyes and 1 place to the right of D's hair.

3. C's mouth is 2 places to the left of his nose.

4. B's hair is 1 place to the right of A's eyes.

Can you find the correct hair, eyes, nose, and mouth for each person?

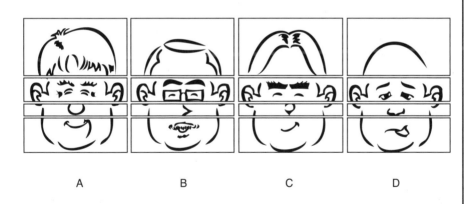

A   B   C   D

Answer on page 179.

Musicians Letterbox

The letters in T REX can be found in boxes 5, 15, 16 and 18, but not necessarily in that order. Similarly, the letters in all the musicians' names can be found in the boxes indicated. Your task is to insert all the letters of the alphabet into the boxes. If you do this correctly, the shaded cells will reveal the name of a rock group.

Hint: Look for words that share a single letter. For example, DANA shares an **A** with CREAM and a **D** with DRIFTERS. By comparing the number lists, you can deduce the box numbers.

BEATLES: 5, 7, 9, 11, 15 & 22

BEN E KING: 6, 10, 11, 12, 15 & 23

BON JOVI: 2, 4, 11, 12, 17 & 23

BOY GEORGE: 10, 11, 15, 16, 17 & 19

BUDDY HOLLY: 1, 7, 11, 13, 17, 19 & 21

CREAM: 9, 15, 16, 20 & 24

DANA: 9, 12 & 13

DRIFTERS: 5, 13, 15, 16, 22, 23 & 25

ELTON JOHN: 1, 2, 5, 7, 12, 15 & 17

PINK FLOYD: 6, 7, 12, 13, 17, 19, 23, 25 & 26

QUEEN: 8, 12, 15 & 21

T REX: 5, 15, 16 & 18

WIZZARD: 3, 9, 13, 14, 16 & 23

ZOMBIES: 3, 11, 15, 17, 20, 22 & 23

1	2	3	4	5	6	7	8	9	10	11	12	13

14	15	16	17	18	19	20	21	22	23	24	25	26

Answer on page 179.

Fitting Words

In this miniature crossword, the clues are listed randomly and are numbered for convenience only. It is up to you to figure out the placement of the 9 answers. To help you out, we've inserted 1 letter in the grid, and this is the only occurrence of that letter in the puzzle.

1. Hangs on to

2. Skin soother

3. E.T., e.g.

4. Finishes

5. Financial institution

6. Desert wanderer

7. Pile

8. "Newsweek" rival

9. Soak in the tub

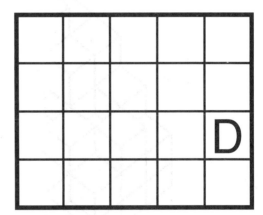

What's the Time?

How many minutes is it before 12 noon if 28 minutes ago it was 3 times as many minutes past 10 A.M.?

Cube Count

How many individual cubes are in this configuration? Assume all rows and columns are complete unless you actually see them end.

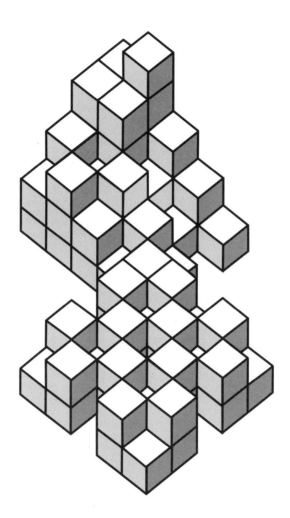

Answer on page 180.

Battle Boats

Place each ship in the fleet located at right within the grid. They may be placed horizontally or vertically, but they can't touch each other (not even diagonally). Numbers reveal the ship segments located in that row or column.

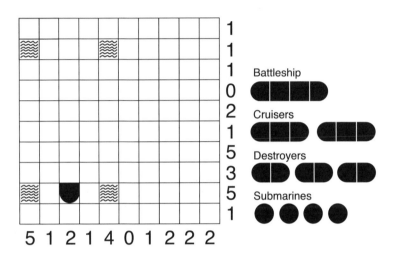

1
1
1
0
2
1
5
3
5
1

5 1 2 1 4 0 1 2 2 2

Battleship

Cruisers

Destroyers

Submarines

Trivia on the Brain

Your brain actually grows, if you put it to use. Brain scans of cab drivers in London showed that the hippocampus—the part of the brain that helps us navigate—was larger than those of other people.

Hitori

The object of this puzzle is to have a number appear only once in each row and column. By shading a number cell, you are effectively removing that number from its row and column. There's a catch though: Shaded number cells are never adjacent to one another in a row or column.

1	2	4	3	7	5	1	8
1	5	3	8	5	1	6	4
4	1	5	3	2	3	6	6
3	6	2	5	4	8	7	1
7	5	1	7	8	2	4	3
6	3	5	2	5	4	7	7
2	4	8	8	6	4	1	5
5	2	6	1	6	7	3	6

Answer on page 180.

Get It Straight

Don't get too caught up in all the twists and turns as you negotiate your way to the center of this intricate labyrinth.

Word Columns

Find the humorous limerick by Anthony Euwer by using the letters directly below each of the blank squares. Each letter is used only once. A black square indicates the end of a word.

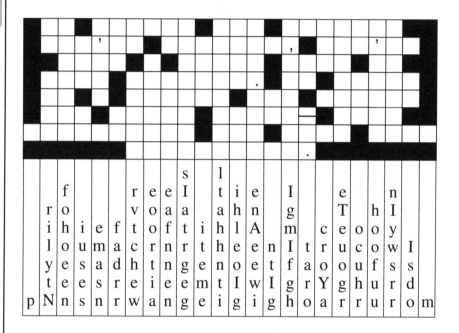

Trivia on the Brain

Did you know that your skin weighs about twice as much as your brain?

Answer on page 180.

Masyu

Masyu has a simple goal: to draw a single, nonintersecting loop through all of the pearls on the grid.

There are 2 rules according to the color of the pearl:

Black pearls: A line must enter and exit at right angles from the pearl. It must also extend straight for 2 squares in the chosen direction.

White pearls: A line goes straight through each pearl and must turn immediately before or after. It is optional for the line to turn both before and after.

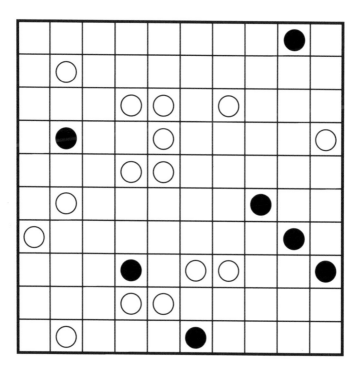

Odd One Out

Can you determine which of the words below is the odd one out?

Hint: Think about structures and meanings.

WE'LL   HE'LL   I'LL   YOU'LL

L'adder

Starting at the bottom rung, use the numbers 1 through 9 to add up to the top number. Numbers can only be used once. There's a catch though: The precise sums must be met along the way.

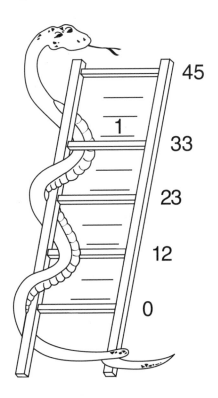

45

1   33

23

12

0

Answers on page 180.

Hobby Horse

Which of these is not an anagram for a pleasant hobby?

A. PIANIST IRON

B. HAPPY HOG ROT

C. ENDING RAG

D. DOG WON VICAR

Stick Figures (Part I)

Study the figures below for one minute. Then turn the page for a memory challenge.

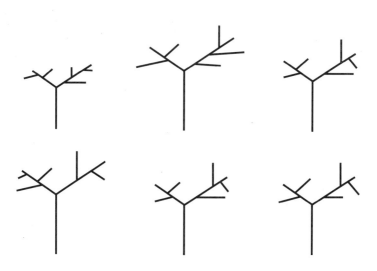

Stick Figures (Part II)

(Do not read this until you have read page 91!)

Can you identify the figure that appeared twice on the previous page?

A.   B.   C.

D.   E.

Rhyme Time

Each clue leads to a 2-word answer that rhymes, such as BIG PIG or STABLE TABLE. The numbers in parentheses after the clue give the number of letters in each word. For example, "cookware taken from the oven (3, 3)" would be "hot pot."

1. Sagacious fellows (4, 4): _____

2. Grassy city area with no illumination (4, 4): _____
_____

3. Having soreness while gathering fallen leaves (6, 6): _____
_____

4. Justification for a turncoat's crime (7, 6): _____
_____

5. Biblical twin's teeter-totters (5, 7): _____
_____

Answers on page 180.

Hamster Treadmill

CREATIVE THINKING SPATIAL VISUALIZATION VISUAL LOGIC

Only one of these exercise devices allows the hamster to run freely without the belts getting stuck. Is it device A or B?

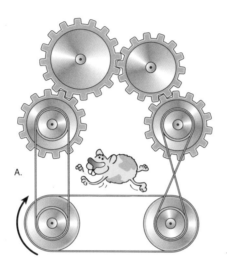

A.

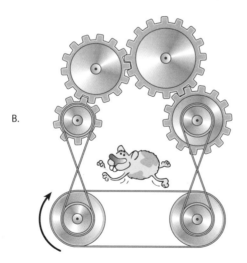

B.

Answer on page 181.

Hashi

Each circle represents an island, with the number inside indicating the number of bridges connected to it. Draw bridges between islands using the number given. There can be no more than 2 bridges going in the same direction, and there must be a continuous path connecting all islands. Bridges can only be vertical or horizontal and may not cross islands or other bridges. We've drawn some bridges to get you started.

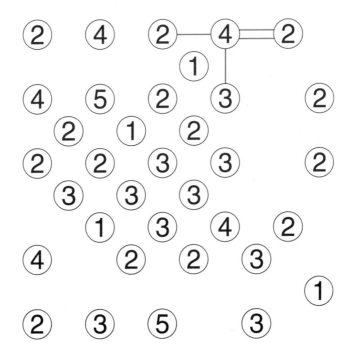

Answer on page 181.

Kakuro

Place a number from 1 through 9 in each empty cell so that the sum of each vertical or horizontal run (rows and columns extending from already numbered cells) equals the number at the top or on the left of that run. Numbers may not be repeated in any run, and runs end at dark-colored squares.

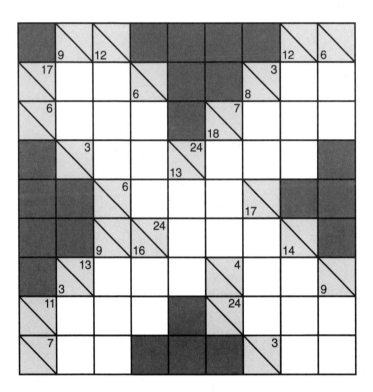

Clapboard

Like a crossword puzzle, the goal here is to find the word or words best suited for the given clues. But unlike a crossword, there are no boxes that separate one word from another. In fact, words on the same line often blend together here. The letters at the end of one word sometimes form the beginning of the next, but only on the same line; words never carry over from one row or column to the next.

Across
1. Adhere
6. Jabbers
8. Inked
14. More creepy
15. Peruse
16. Lorna _____
17. Making possible
19. Roses' home
20. Brothers and sisters
21. Rosebud, e.g.
22. Bad-mouth
23. Appears
26. Merges
28. Kitchen device
29. Bread or whiskey
32. Passover feast
33. Glued to the tube
35. Road surface
36. Cambodian currency
37. Abound
39. Naturalist John
40. Big _____

41. Wind blasts
45. Prince Valiant's son
47. Requisite
48. Faulty fireworks
49. A winter woe
50. Small amount, Greek
52. Down in the dumps
53. International easing
56. Egghead
58. Accomplished
59. Morning moisture
61. Child's card game
62. The start of something bigger
63. Island instrument
64. Sea eagle
65. Type of orange
67. Entices
71. Sandra or Ruby

72. Per pop
73. Zeus' wife
74. Summer cooler
75. Dutch commune
76. Snaky shape
77. "A Streetcar Named Desire" role
78. Meeting manager

Down
1. Average grades
2. Stalin's predecessor
3. Saver's device
4. Pen points
5. Uri who claims to be psychic
6. Sign of the Ram
7. Oregon city
8. Droop
9. Cantor and Lupino
10. Al or Tipper
11. Protuberance
12. Foe

13. Hard to penetrate
18. Put up with
19. Present
20. Keep up
21. Plant part
22. Downturn
23. Males only affairs
24. Poetic contraction
25. Goddess of discord
27. Poetic contraction
28. Announced
30. Still

31. Golfer Ernie
33. Regrets
34. Prig
35. Neap or ebb
36. He's in charge
38. Tolkien creature
39. Honey-based liquor
40. Boorish
42. Mexicali mister
43. Vietnamese holiday
44. Doesn't dele
46. Shad delicacy
48. June celebrant
49. WWII camp
51. Forest units

52. Because
54. Cote denizen
55. Digit
56. Museum display
57. Supplements the hard way
58. Mild expletive
59. Actress Arlene
60. Daredevil Knievel
62. Boorish
66. Important time
68. Stimpy's cartoon buddy
69. Actor Byrnes
70. Ross, e.g.

1	2	3	4	5	6	7	8	9	10	11	12	13
14				15			16					
17	18					19						
20		21			22		23	24	25			
26	27		28						29	30	31	
32			33		34	35		36 A	R	I	E	L
37	38	39		40		41			42	43	44	
45	46	47		48			49					
50		51	52		53	54			55			
56	57		58		59	60	61		62			
63		64		65			66	67		68	69	70
71		72			73			74		75		
76		77				78						

Answers on page 181.

Magic Square

The numbers 2, 4, 6, 8, and 10 should appear only once in every row, column, and long diagonal. Some of the squares have already been filled in. Can you fill in the rest?

		10		6
			2	
2	4			
10			8	

Trivia on the Brain

On average, the male brain is slightly bigger than the female brain. Each person's brain is about the size of their two fists.

Answer on page 181.

Flip the Cards

Three cards have been laid out, each marked with a letter on one side and a number or symbol on the other. To make sure that every card with an F has an 8 on the other side, and that no F cards have a star symbol on the other side, which cards need to be turned over?

A. All 3 cards

B. The card on the left and the card on the right

C. The card on the right and the card in the middle

D. The card on the left and the card in the middle

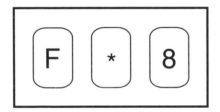

Name That Name (Part I)

Carefully study the names and occupations below for 2 minutes before turning the page for a memory challenge. Some of these names can be misleading.

Tony Sparrow	Entertainer
Samuel Painter	Carpenter
Frank Cook	Chauffeur
Samantha Kitchen	Tailor
Alan Wood	Baker
Annette Driver	Cook
Julia Singer	Ornithologist

Name That Name (Part II)

(Do not read this until you have read page 99!)

Can you fill in the 8 missing pieces of information from the previous page?

Missing Surnames: Wood, Painter, Driver, and Kitchen.

Missing Professions: Ornithologist, entertainer, baker, and chauffeur.

First Name	Surname	Profession
Tony	Sparrow	
Samuel		Carpenter
Frank	Cook	
Samantha		Tailor
Alan		
Annette		Cook
Julia	Singer	

Word Ladder

Using the clues along the way, change just one letter on each line to go from the top word to the bottom word. Do not change the order of the letters. You must have a common English word at each step.

SLED

_____

_____

_____ different colors

_____

_____ oversize

LUGE

Answers on page 181.

Digital Sudoku

Fill in the grid so that each row, column, and 2 by 3 block contains the numbers 1 through 6 exactly once. Numbers are in digital form, and some segments have already been filled in.

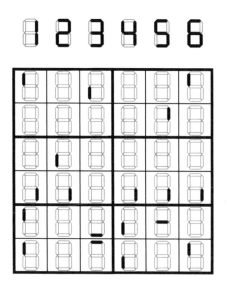

Crypto-Logic

Each of the numbers in the sequence below represents a letter. Use the mathematical clues to determine which number stands for which letter, and reveal the encrypted word.

Hint: Remember that the sign / indicates "divided by."

6 4 9 1 5 7

Clues:

A = 8	4I = E	R / 2 = U
A / B = 4	3E / 2 = G	R − 1 = N
A / 2B = 2I	G + E = R	N − 2I = S

Cross-Math

Place the digits 1 through 9 in the empty white squares so that the 3 horizontal and 3 vertical equations are true. Each digit will be used exactly once. Calculations are done from left to right and from top to bottom.

	−		÷		=	2
+		+		×		
	×		+		=	20
÷		+		−		
	+		+		=	20
=		=		=		
3		12		6		

⚙ Trivia on the Brain

The spinal cord is like an old telephone switchboard. Every message going into or coming out of the brain goes through the nerves of the spinal cord.

Answer on page 182.

Grid Fill

LANGUAGE PLANNING

To complete this puzzle, place the given letters and words into the shapes on this grid. Words and letters will run across, down, and wrap around each shape. When the grid is filled, each row will contain one of the following words: attire, blinds, finite, garage, hourly, lapsed, overly.

1. D, I

2. AR, FI, HO, ND

3. LAG, SLY, TEE

4. BOAT, RELY, SAGE

5. LIVER

6. TURNIP

Fitting Words

In this miniature crossword, the clues are listed randomly and are numbered for convenience only. It is up to you to figure out the placement of the 9 answers. To help you out, we've inserted 1 letter in the grid, and this is the only occurrence of that letter in the puzzle.

1. "Nevermore" speaker

2. In the know

3. Length times width, for a rectangle

4. Picnic locale

5. Fully grown cygnet

6. "Poppycock!"

7. Proceed specifically

8. Work, as dough

9. Possess

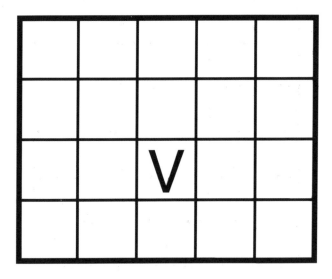

Answer on page 182.

Maggie's List

Maggie was looking at a long list of sequential whole numbers. At one point, she noticed the sequence included these numbers:

207　216　225　234　243　252

Which one of the following is a number Maggie would most likely see if she continued looking down the list?

A. 169

B. 1,248

C. 891

D. 1,000,001

Circular Memory (Part I)

Study the circles below for 1 minute, then turn the page for a memory challenge.

Answer on page 182.

MEMORY

Circular Memory (Part II)

(Do not read this until you have read page 105!)

Can you identify which of these groups of two circles were in the same order on previous page?

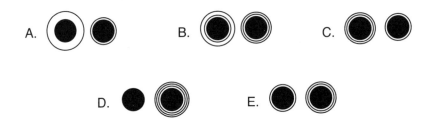

A.   B.   C.

D.   E.

LOGIC

LANGUAGE

Party Time

Cryptograms are messages in substitution code. Break the code to read the humorous statement. For example, THE SMART CAT might become FVO QWGDF JGF if **F** is substituted for **T, V** for **H, O** for **E,** and so on.

OUCUSNM JXOEHSXFNM

PXBWSUO DUSU XRCXEUV EH N

GNSEA. UXROEUXR ONXV XE DHWMV

IU SUMNEXCUMA UNOA EH NEEURV.

OFJWIUSE ONXV JU'V FHKU, IWE

EJUSU DNO OHKUEJXRB JU JNV EH

PXRXOJ PXSOE. VS. TUQAMM DNO HP

EDH KXRVO...

Answers on page 182.

Star Power

Fill in each empty square in the grid so that each star is surrounded by the numbers 1 through 8 with no repeats.

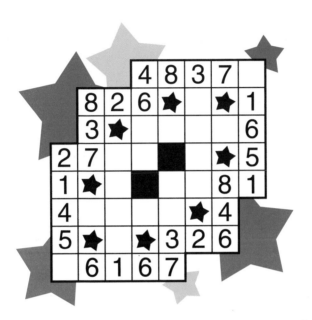

Trivia on the Brain

Your brain is part of your body, so it needs to be physically fit as well as mentally strong. Physical exercise is important to keep your brain in tip-top shape.

Uncrossed Paths

Draw lines to like symbols (triangle to triangle, star to star) without any line crossing another line. A black line cannot be crossed, while a striped line can be crossed only once.

VISUAL LOGIC

SPATIAL VISUALIZATION

CREATIVE THINKING

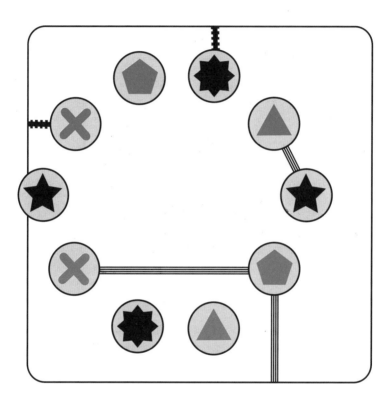

108

Answer on page 182.

Hashi

Each circle represents an island, with the number inside indicating the number of bridges connected to it. Draw bridges between islands using the number given. There can be no more than 2 bridges going in the same direction, and there must be a continuous path connecting all islands. Bridges can only be vertical or horizontal and may not cross islands or other bridges. We've drawn some bridges to get you started.

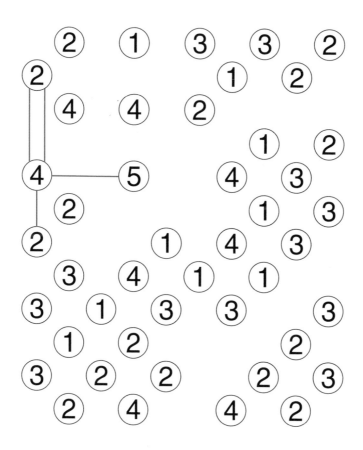

Perfect Score

Make 3 successful hits so that the sum of the numbers is 100. Double and triple scores do not apply. Numbers may be used more than once.

Trivia on the Brain

Your brain uses fatty acids from fats to create the specialized cells that allow you to think and feel.

Answer on page 183.

Word Columns

Find the hidden book excerpt and its author by using the letters directly below each of the blank squares. Each letter is used only once. A black square indicates the end of a word.

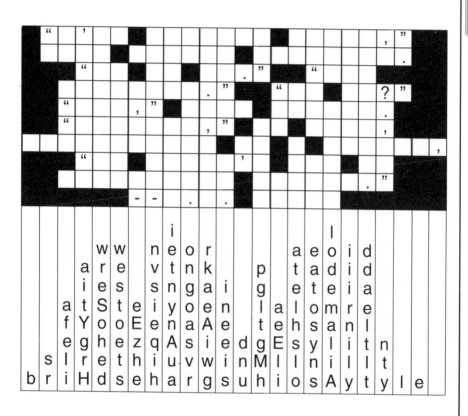

Word Ladder

Use the clues to change just one letter on each line to go from the top word to the bottom word. Do not change the order of the letters. You must have a common English word at each step.

STRAP

_____ what a scarecrow is made of

_____ to throw about the place

_____ no use without a driver

_____ a green sod

_____ Go away!

_____ a Rugby formation

_____ anti-viral

STRUM

Twenty-four Jumble

Arrange the numbers and math signs in this cornucopia to come up with the number 24.

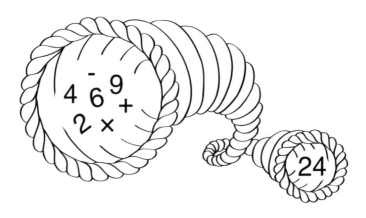

Answers on page 183.

Round and Round (Part 1)

Study the illustrations for 2 minutes, and remember the names of the objects. Then turn the page for a memory challenge.

Raise Your Puzzle Potential

Round and Round (Part II)

(Do not read this until you have read page 113!)

Which of the items below were pictured on page 113?

Frying pan

Smiley face

Earth

Cookie

Marble

Pizza

Ship's wheel

Pancake

Baseball

Basketball

Golf ball

Soccer ball

Stopwatch

Answers on page 183.

Marbles

Place 12 marbles into the grid without having any touch one another, not even diagonally. There are some walls, represented by thick lines, that block the view of the marbles. Marbles must not "see" each other in a horizontal or vertical direction. We've placed 1 to get you started.

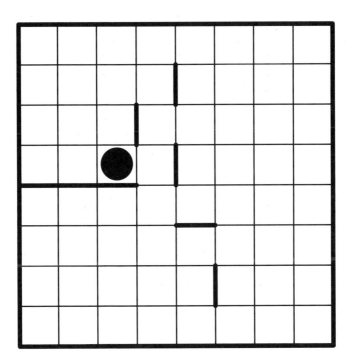

Name Calling

Decipher the encoded words in the quip below using the numbers and letters on the phone pad. Remember that each number can stand for 3 or 4 possible letters.

Don't 7–3–5–6–4–2–3 at your enemy's 3–2–5–5, but don't 7–8–7–4 to pick him up 3–4–8–4–3–7.

Trivia on the Brain

The word "cerebellum" comes from the Latin words meaning "little brain."

Answer on page 183.

Buried Nuts

Sally the squirrel has buried nuts in various locations, but she has forgotten the details. In her attempt to make a list, only 1 item in each column is correctly positioned, although each item is in the correct column. The following facts are certain about the correct order:

1. River is 2 places above dogwood and 3 places above 7 nuts.

2. Neither lake nor wood are fifth.

3. The 10 nuts amount is 1 place below beech and 1 place above lake.

4. Neither 10 nor 15 nuts are in fifth place.

5. Neither the ash nor the elm is second.

6. The 8 nuts amount is 1 place below garden and 3 places above fir.

Can you give the tree, location, and number of nuts buried for each position?

	Tree	Location	No. Nuts
1	ash	park	5
2	beech	garden	7
3	cedar	river	8
4	dogwood	wood	10
5	elm	fence	12
6	fir	lake	15

Missing Connections

It's a crossword without the clues! Use the letters below to fill in the empty spaces in the crossword grid. When you are finished, you'll have words that read both across and down, crossword-style.

A A A A B B B D D D E E F I

K M N P P R Q S T T U U X Y Z

Answer on page 183.

You Are Here

…and the taxi meter is ticking. This professional building is a maze of corridors and cubicles. Elevators are local or express only; there are no stairs. And over-stressed office workers won't give you directions to the exit. Why, oh why, did you ever come in here? Doesn't matter now—time to get moving!

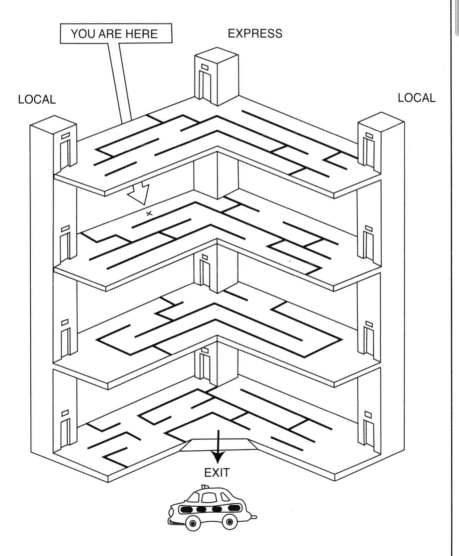

Traffic Light

Across

1. Shingle words
6. Leaning Tower's locale
10. Atlas pages
14. When repeated, a Yale cheer
15. Baldwin of "Prelude to a Kiss"
16. Slangy suffix
17. Shaq's game: sl.
18. Juror, in theory
19. Comparable
20. 1971 Richard Thomas film
23. Keep them about you
24. Peter, Paul, and Mary
25. Hall of Famer, e.g.
28. Midler of "The Rose"
30. Not for kids
31. German auto
32. Zimbalist drama, with "The"
35. Way in "The Wizard of Oz"
39. NBC weekend comedy: abbr.
40. Rubik creation
41. "Biography" network
42. Clumps of grass
44. Highly valued
45. Andre of the courts
48. Hammerhead part
49. Dr. Seuss book
55. In case
56. "Damn Yankees" girl
57. Bent out of shape

58. Mayberry jailbird
59. Contest for two
60. Forbidden acts
61. Ending with silver or soft
62. Flower supporter
63. Church areas

Down

1. E.g., e.g.
2. Half of Hamlet's question:
3. Unit of laundry
4. "No trouble to report"
5. Enter: 2 wds.
6. Mamas' mates
7. "Why should _____ you?"
8. Appear
9. Type of word puzzle
10. Nasty sort
11. Actor Alan
12. Decimal dot
13. "Yesterday" and "Tomorrow"
21. From Jan. 1 to now: abbr.
22. Informer
25. Produces eggs
26. Forbidden fruit site
27. Coastal bird
28. City outskirts, briefly
29. Singer Adams
31. Go to the edge of
32. Winkler role, with "the"
33. Expressed, as a welcome
34. Picked out of a lineup
36. "The Bank Dick" actor

37. Tolstoy's Anna
38. Bit of precipitation
42. Fly in the tropics
43. PT boats are in it
44. Soup legume
45. Radiant
46. Actress Garbo

47. Norse race
48. Biblical poem
50. Joint inflammation
51. Euphoria
52. First name in fairy tales
53. Stick _____ in the water
54. Tough spot

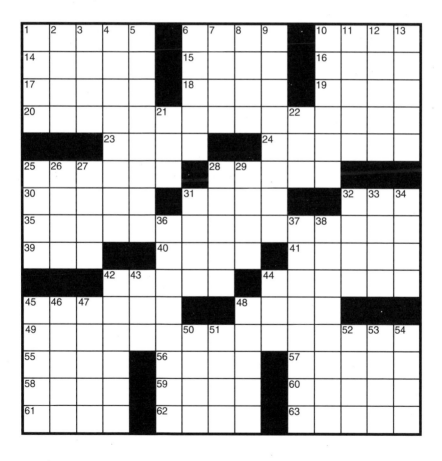

Odd-Even Logidoku

PLANNING

LOGIC

The numbers 1 through 9 are to appear once in every row, column, long diagonal, irregular shape, and 3 by 3 grid. Cells marked with the letter **E** contain even numbers. From the numbers given, can you complete the puzzle?

	E		E		E		E	
1	E			E	E		9	E
	E	E					E	E
E		E	E		E			
	7		E			E	2	E
E		E		E	5			E
		E	8	E		E		
E	E				E	E		
6		3		E		4	E	

Trivia on the Brain

In 1504, Leonardo da Vinci produced wax casts of the ventricles of the human brain.

Answer on page 184.

Mondrianize It!

ANALYSIS | LOGIC

Inspired by the artwork of Belgian artist Piet Mondrian, these puzzles consist of stars and circles. Using the checkered pattern as a guide, draw in lines so that each star is in its own square, and each circle in its own rectangle.

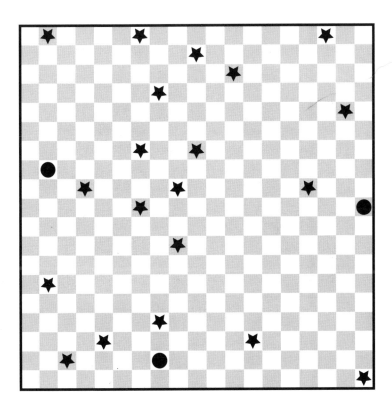

Circular Reasoning

That's what you'll need to get from the top dot to the bottom one in this sort-of-circular maze.

Answer on page 184.

ABCD

Every cell in this grid contains one of 4 letters: A, B, C, or D. No letter can be horizontally or vertically adjacent to itself. The tables above and to the left of the grid indicate how many times each letter appears in that column or row.

Can you complete the grid?

LOGIC PLANNING

				A	B	C	D
			A	2	0	2	3	2	2	2	0	0
			B	0	3	2	2	1	2	2	2	2
			C	1	3	1	1	2	1	1	2	3
A	B	C	D	3	0	1	0	1	1	1	2	1

A	B	C	D									
2	3	2	2									
4	3	2	0									
1	0	4	4									
2	3	2	2									
3	3	3	0									
1	4	2	2								D	

Quic-Kross

LANGUAGE

GENERAL KNOWLEDGE

This is a crossword puzzle with a twist. Use the clues to solve the puzzle. When complete, the circled letters will spell out a "mystery word."

Across

1. Having weapons
2. Withstand
3. Spoon gravy on
4. Discharge weapon
5. Precious stone

Down

6. Joined system
7. Compensate for
8. Take along
9. Flock of young
10. Star constellation ("Bull")

Mystery word clue: Remission of sin

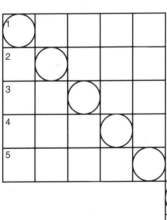
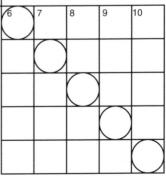

Answers on page 185.

Word Paths

Each of these word paths contains a familiar saying. To figure out the saying, read freely from letter to letter, starting with the letter indicated by the arrow. Some letters will be used more than once, and you can move both forward and backward along the straight lines. The blanks indicate the number of letters in each word of the saying.

1.

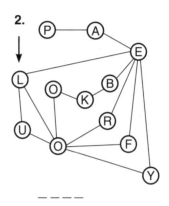

_ _ _ _ _   _ _ _
_ _ _ _   _ _ _

2.

_ _ _ _
_ _ _ _ _ _   _ _ _
_ _ _ _

3.

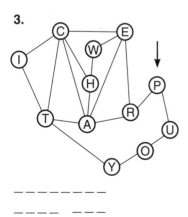

_ _ _ _ _ _ _ _
_ _ _ _   _ _ _
_ _ _ _ _ _

4.

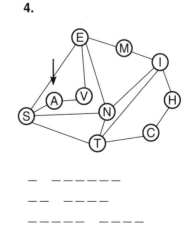

_   _ _ _ _ _
_ _   _ _ _ _
_ _ _ _ _   _ _ _ _

Red, White, Blue, and Green

Two reds, 2 whites, 2 blues, and 2 greens are to be placed in every row, column, and long diagonal in the grid on the next page. The following clues will help you place them.

2. The blues are separated by 6 cells.

3. The pattern of colors takes the form ABCDDCBA.

5. The whites are not adjacent.

6. The reds cannot be found in cells E, F, G, or H.

7. The greens are separated by 2 cells; the whites are not adjacent.

8. The pattern of colors takes the form ABCABCDD.

A. The blues are separated by 5 cells; 1 white is enclosed by a blue and a red; the other by a green and a red.

B. The reds are separated by 5 cells; the whites are separated by 5 cells.

C. The reds cannot be found in cells 1, 2, 3, or 4.

D. Each green is directly above each red.

E. Each green is directly above each white.

F. One red is directly enclosed by the blues.

G. The reds are separated by 5 cells.

H. The greens cannot be found in cells 1, 2, 3, or 4; the reds cannot be found in cells 5, 6, 7, or 8; the blues are separated by 4 cells.

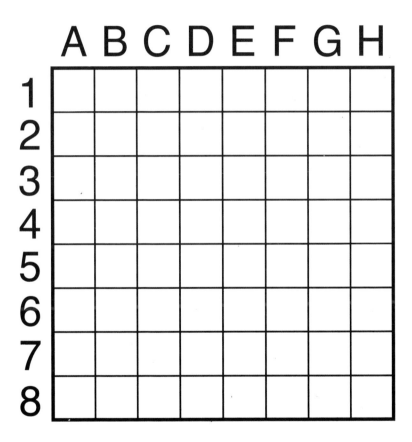

Hitori

The object of this puzzle is to have a number appear only once in each row and column. By shading a number cell, you are effectively removing that number from its row and column. There's a catch though: Shaded number cells are never adjacent to one another in a row or column.

4	4	1	8	5	2	7	5
7	5	3	2	6	3	1	4
8	4	3	7	5	5	6	1
4	6	3	5	4	8	4	2
5	3	8	8	7	1	2	4
8	1	5	3	5	7	2	6
3	5	7	4	1	6	8	5
6	8	4	8	2	2	5	1

 Trivia on the Brain

From early childhood through puberty, synapses in the human neocortex are lost at a rate of 100,000 synapses per second.

Answer on page 185.

Grid Fill

To complete this puzzle, place the given letters and words into the shapes on this grid. Words and letters will run across, down, and wrap around each shape. When the grid is filled, each row will contain one of the following words: arches, closet, inside, salute, sodium, strand, talons.

1. I, R, T

2. RC, SC

3. AOL, SUM

4. DOSE, EDEN, ENDS, SALT, SILO, UTAH

5. SAINT

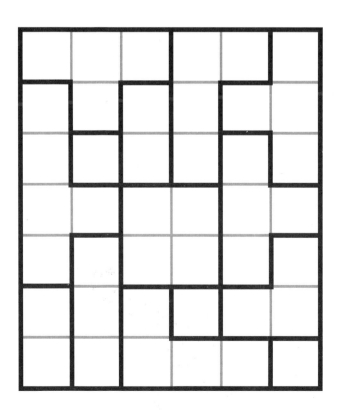

Answer on page 185.

Word-a-Maze: Avian Home

Travel in sequence through the puzzle on the next page from the left side to the right, using each numbered clue to determine the correct word. Connect adjacent words together with a common letter to proceed through the maze. Some letters are already given. The first and last words tie into the title.

1. Feathered creatures

2. Categorize

3. Canvas dwelling

4. Slow run

5. Verbalize

6. Rabbi approved

7. Interpret writing

8. Patriarch

9. Debonair

10. Grind teeth

11. Chopped meat

12. Float

13. Fish eggs

14. Completion

15. Scuba _____

16. Guaranteed again

17. Form of tobacco

18. Not ornate

19. Stack together

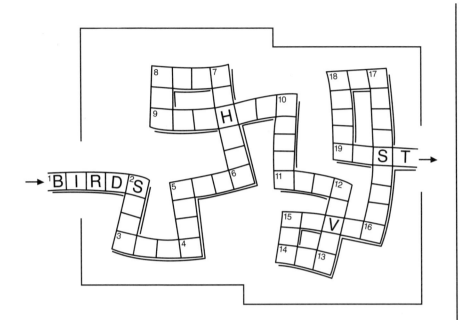

Trivia on the Brain

What we know about the brain comes from studies of brain tissues and of behavior, and of how the first relates to the second.

Code-doku

Solve this puzzle just as you would a sudoku. Use deductive logic to complete the grid so that each row, each column, and each 3 by 3 box contains each of the letters ABCEKLPRU in some order. The solution is unique.

When you have completed the puzzle, unscramble those 9 letters to reveal the name of a Nobel-prize-winning author.

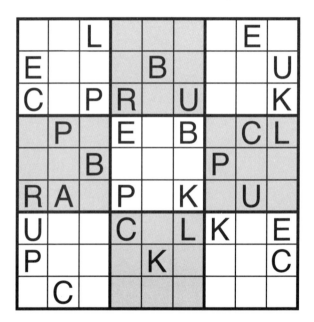

Answer: _____

Wacky Wordy

Can you "read" the phrase below?

JUDADDGE

Answers on page 185.

Hashi

Each circle represents an island, with the number inside indicating the number of bridges connected to it. Draw bridges between islands using the number given. There can be no more than 2 bridges going in the same direction, and there must be a continuous path connecting all islands. Bridges can only be vertical or horizontal and may not cross islands or other bridges. We've drawn some bridges to get you started.

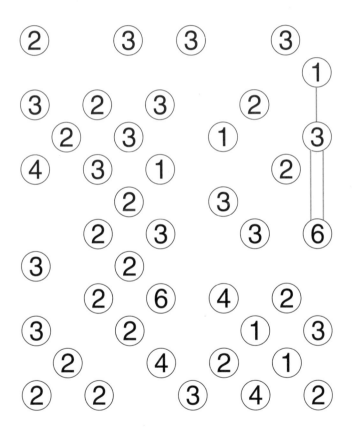

1-2-3

Place the numbers 1, 2, or 3 in the circles below. The challenge is to have only these 3 numbers in each connected row and column—no number should repeat. Any combination is allowed.

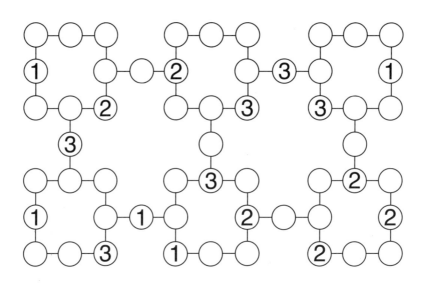

Answer on page 186.

Kakuro

Place a number from 1 through 9 in each empty cell so that the sum of each vertical or horizontal run (rows and columns extending from already numbered cells) equals the number at the top or on the left of that run. Numbers may not be repeated in any run, and runs end at dark-colored squares.

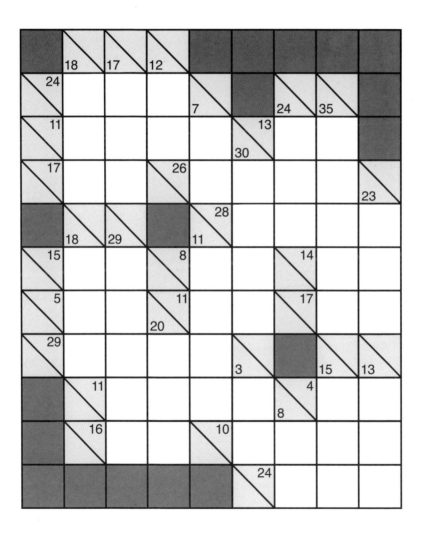

Word Jigsaw

Fit the pieces into the frame to form common, uncapitalized words reading across and down. There's no need to rotate the pieces; they'll fit as shown, with each piece used exactly once.

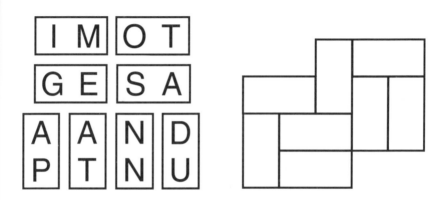

Tamagram

Find a way to define the word and style of the letters below, and then rearrange the letters of that to form a 9-letter word. LLL, for example, is THREE L'S, which is an anagram of SHELTER.

END

Answers on page 186.

Vex-a-Gon

Place the numbers 1 through 6 into the triangles of each hexagon. The numbers may be in any order but they do not repeat within each hexagon shape.

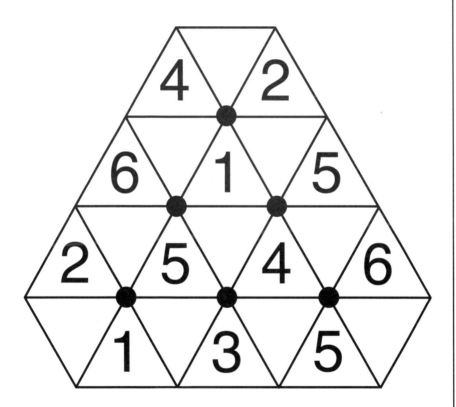

The Yellow-Brick Road

LOGIC

ANALYSIS

The yellow-brick road splits into the green- and the red-brick roads, which lead respectively to the red city and the green city. In one of these cities, everyone tells the truth; in the other, everyone lies. You want to get to the city of truth. Two people are waiting at the fork in the road, one from each city. You can ask one person this question: "If I were to ask the other person what you would tell me if I asked you which road leads to the city of truth, what would they tell me?" If they answer, "They would tell you that I would tell you to take the red road," which road should I take?

A. The red road

B. The green road

C. It is impossible to know

Trivia on the Brain

Your memory can be divided into three types: long-term memory, short-term memory, and immediate memory.

Answer on page 186.

Arrow Web

Shade in some of the arrows so that each arrow in the grid points to exactly 1 shaded arrow.

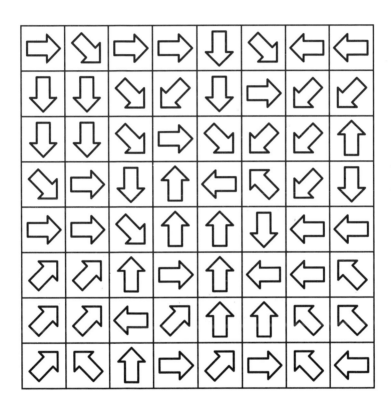

Togs

Across

1. Some soft drinks
6. Massachusetts Cape
9. Sao _____, Brazil
14. Mennonite group
15. Buck's mate
16. Muscular strength
17. "Calm down!"
20. A deadly sin
21. World-weary
22. Sup
23. Command to Rover
24. Saw eye-to-eye
26. Wizardry
30. A Stooge
32. Gas company bought by BP
33. Oklahoma city
34. Cleopatra's undoing
37. "By the _____ ... " (words just before pronouncing a marriage)
40. 9-digit ID: abbr.
41. A horse of a different color
42. Not over
43. Quality of a saint
44. Advantage
45. French Foreign _____
48. Flexible fish
50. Do pressing work?
51. Requires
54. Palm starch
58. It might contain the author's biography

61. Wally Cleaver's friend
62. Sleep state, for short
63. 2:1, say
64. Bowling alley button
65. "The Star-Spangled Banner" land
66. Observe Yom Kippur

Down

1. Birthday dessert
2. Broken mirror, say
3. Ukraine's capital
4. Spot
5. Hardly outgoing
6. Of age
7. Ibsen's heroine
8. Capone's bane
9. Letter before omega
10. Hang on a clothesline
11. Loosen a shoelace
12. Sierra _____, Africa
13. Held the deed to
18. Ornamental sash
19. Funeral parlor's vehicle
23. Many a November birth
25. Moderate, as a progression
26. Cartographer's creations
27. "Famous" cookie maker
28. Bridesmaid's purchase
29. Commit a hockey no-no
30. Hot-blooded
31. Voice below soprano
33. Camper's abode

34. "...ifs, _____ or buts"
35. "Peter Pan" villain
36. Sassy
38. Capital of Austria
39. Election winners
43. Little finger
45. Reading matter, to Nero
46. Wear away
47. Merchandise
48. Abnormal plant swelling

49. Winter hours in NYC
52. Hosiery shade
53. Barely makes, with "out"
54. Venetian blind part
55. Jaguar or Mustang
56. Mild joke reaction
57. Slender woodwind
59. Deep black
60. Bikini part

Tessellated Floor

Show how the five pieces (A. through E.) can form the mosaic floor below. Pieces can be rotated, but they do not overlap and are not mirrored.

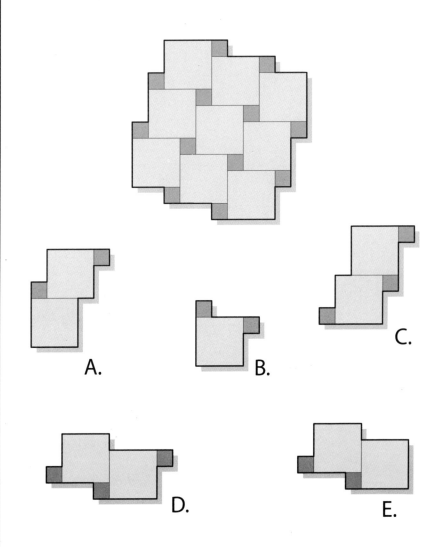

A.

B.

C.

D.

E.

Answer on page 187.

Add It Up

COMPUTATION LOGIC

Fill each square in the grid with a digit from 1 through 9. When the numbers in each row are added, you should arrive at the total in the right hand column. When the numbers in each column are added, you should arrive at the total on the bottom line. The numbers in each long diagonal must add to the totals in the upper and lower right corners.

											63
	5	8	3	2	2		5	1	8		47
1		5		2	1	6	5	8			42
	3		2	1	6	5	8	1	2		39
1	6	2		8		7		9	5		46
9	1	4	3	1				3	9		38
5		9	1		5	4	6		7		53
8		6	9		6	2	8		2		62
6	2			7	4	7	7	1	8		46
7		2	5		8		2	3	7		47
4	3	8	4	2		1		5			44
55	42	49	36	36	42	42	51	45	66	43	

Cluster

Fill in each grape so that the number in descending rows is the total of the neighboring numbers from the row above it. Each grape contains a positive whole number. Numbers can be repeated.

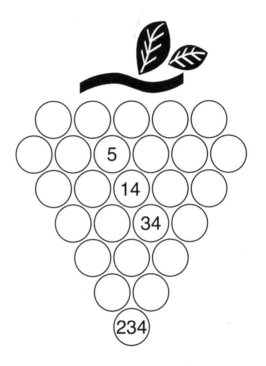

Trivia on the Brain

The first known writing about the human brain was found in ancient Sumerian records from around 4000 B.C.

Answer on page 187.

Marbles

Place 15 marbles into the grid without having any touch one another, not even diagonally. There are some walls, represented by thick lines, that block the view of the marbles. Marbles must not "see" each other in a horizontal or vertical direction. We've placed 1 to get you started.

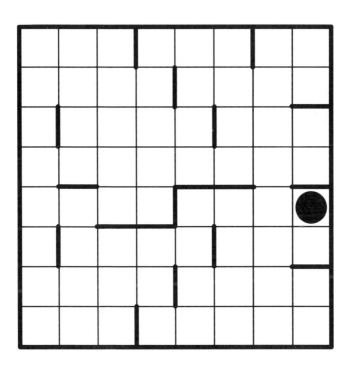

Wacky Wordy

Can you "read" the phrase below?

g   o   e   s

Red, White, Blue, and Green

Two reds, 2 whites, 2 blues, and 2 greens are to be placed in every row, column, and long diagonal in the grid on the next page. The following clues will help you place them.

1. One white is directly enclosed by the reds; the other by the blues.

2. The whites are not adjacent.

3. The greens are adjacent.

4. There are no blues in cells E, F, G, or H; the whites are separated by 6 cells.

7. Each green is immediately left of each blue; the reds are adjacent.

8. The blues, 2 greens, and a red are directly enclosed by the whites.

A. The reds and a blue are directly enclosed by the whites; the greens are not adjacent.

B. There are no reds in cells 1, 2, 3, or 4.

C. Three different colors are directly enclosed by the reds.

D. The reds, a blue, and a green are directly enclosed by the whites.

F. The blues are adjacent.

G. The whites are separated by 6 cells.

H. A green and a white are directly enclosed by the reds.

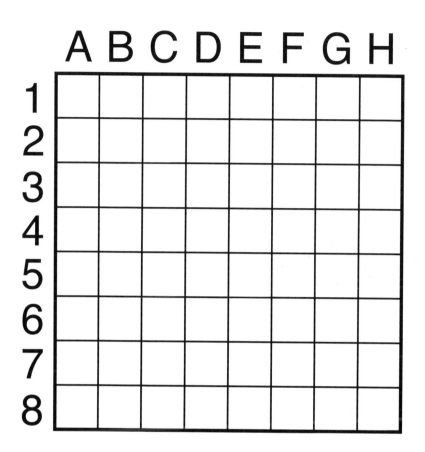

Get It Straight

Don't get too caught up in all the twists and turns as you negotiate your way to the center of this intricate labyrinth.

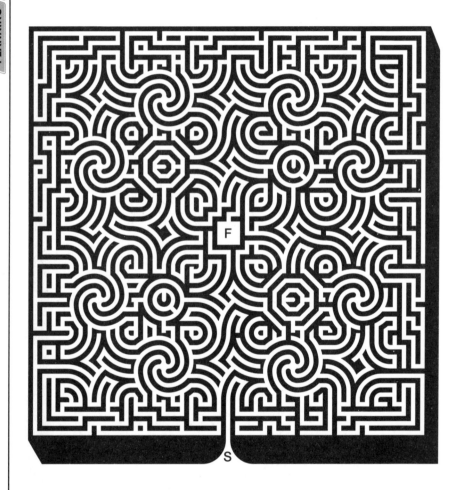

Answer on page 188.

Word Columns

Find the hidden humorous prayer and its author by using the letters directly below each of the blank squares. Each letter is used only once. A black square indicates the end of a word.

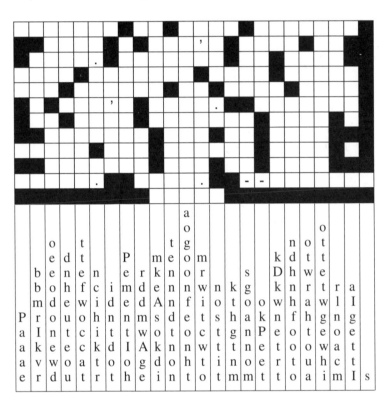

 Trivia on the Brain

Written about 1700 B.C., the Edwin Smith surgical papyrus contains the first recorded use of the word "brain."

Hashi

Each circle represents an island, with the number inside indicating how many bridges are connected to it. Draw bridges between islands using the number given. There can be no more than 2 bridges going in the same direction, and there must be a continuous path connecting all islands. Bridges can only be horizontal or vertical and may not cross over islands or other bridges. We've drawn some bridges to get you started.

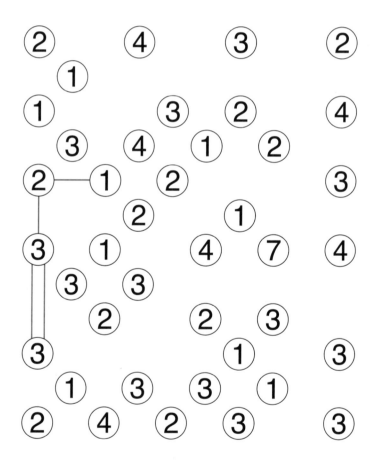

Answer on page 188.

Cross Sums

Use the numbers below to fill in the grid. Each cell at the top of a cross is the sum of numbers below it. So, as seen in the example, A = B + C + D + E.

1 2 3 4 6 7 8 9 10 11 12 28 42

53 54 72 110 125 177

383 428 465 1453

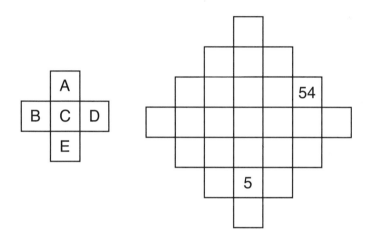

Stopping for Directions (Part I)

Study the arrows below for 20 seconds before turning to the next page for a memory challenge.

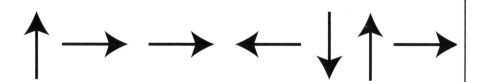

Stopping for Directions (Part II)

(Do not read this until you have read page 153!)

Can you identify which row of arrows appeared on the previous page?

A.

B.

C.

D.

E.

Answer on page 188.

Strings Attached

Below are seven jumbled words or phrases indicated by capital letters. Each is an anagram (rearrangement) of a thing that contains strings. Can you work out all these knots?

"Gather 'round, friends!" said the teacher at the Institute of String Theory. "Here's your challenge: Think of something that has strings, and then form it into an anagram. Who wants to go first?"

"How about SCARLET CAD, a kid's game?" one young genius piped up.

"I have one," a girl in a blue sweater said. "SOPHIE FLING, something you can use to catch a whopper—maybe."

"TRAINEE TOM, something you can make dance," another girl offered.

"ANCIENT TREKS, something you can use on a court," a jock in a letter sweater said.

"TOE BOIL," said another. "It looks better than it sounds!"

"I have no idea what it's for, but a BLIMP LUNE can help you go straight," a student remarked.

"DAMN LION!" a girl yelled. "I mean, pardon my language, but it does make a nice sound."

Number Crossword

ANALYSIS | COMPUTATION

Fill in this crossword with numbers instead of letters. Use the clues to determine which of the numbers 1 through 9 belongs in each square. No zeros are used.

Across

1. The product of its digits is 15

3. A multiple of 29

5. All 5 digits are the same

7. Consecutive odd digits, descending

8. 11-Across times 6-Down

10. A prime number

11. The sum of its digits is 11

Down

1. A multiple of 13

2. 8-Down times 9-Down times 109

3. A palindrome

4. A multiple of 12

6. Consecutive digits, ascending

8. A prime number

9. A prime number

Hint: There is only 1 number with 2 digits that fits 4-Down's description.

1	2		3	4
5		6		
	7			
8				9
10			11	

Answers on page 188.

Star Power

Fill in each empty square in the grid so that each star is surrounded by the numbers 1 through 8 with no repeats.

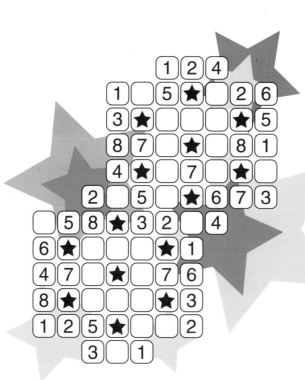

 ## Trivia on the Brain

The outer part of your brain—the cortex—is split into right and left hemispheres, which are connected by a bundle of 50 million neurons.

Codeword

Each letter of the alphabet is hidden in code: They are represented by a random number from 1 through 26. With the letters already given, complete the crossword puzzle with common English words and break the code.

6	26	5	2		26	10	7	24	7	9	24	9
12		10		6		4		26		18		24
4	3	1	23	7	4	13		13	1	4	25	26
15		7		9		13		14		26		3
10	1	3	8	12		12	25	26	3	1	20	26
26				15		16		3		10		12
17	26	9	24	26	3		15	1	9	9	26	24
12		22		6		15		24				2
7	24	26	13	7	21	26		4	9	4	3	14
23		7		26		25		3		23		7
24	12	19	26	23		26	10	26	8	7	1	11
26		22		11		10		9		24		1
6	7	9	14	26	23	9	26		9	26	10	10

1	2	3	4	5	6	7	8	9	10	11	12	13

14	15	16	17	18	19	20	21	22	23	24	25	26
										T		E

Answers on page 189.

No Bones About It

There are 206 bones in a typical adult human skeleton. Can you pick out the fake bone from each list?

1. Wrist bones:
   a) trapezium
   b) trapezoid
   c) capitate
   d) rhomboid

2. Finger bones, or phalanges:
   a) proximal
   b) intermediate
   c) pointal
   d) distal

3. Leg bones:
   a) femur
   b) paella
   c) patella
   d) fibula

4. Ankle bones:
   a) calcaneus
   b) talus
   c) perpendicular
   d) navicular

5. Toe bones, or phalanges:
   a) proximal
   b) intermediate
   c) distal
   d) porkal

6. Vertebrae:
   a) vertical
   b) cervical
   c) lumbar
   d) thoracic

7. Facial bones:
   a) mandible
   b) nasal
   c) palatine
   d) pimpal

8. Skull:
   a) temporal
   b) capital
   c) occipital
   d) frontal

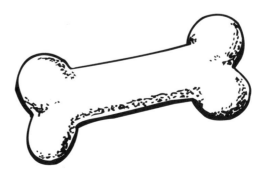

SPATIAL REASONING

PLANNING

Diamond in the Rough

Moving only diagonally, can you find a single, unbroken path from the circle in the upper left corner to the circle in the lower right corner? Your path must move from circle to circle, with 1 twist: You can jump (in a straight line) over any 1 diamond, provided there is a circle on the other side of it. There's only 1 way to do it.

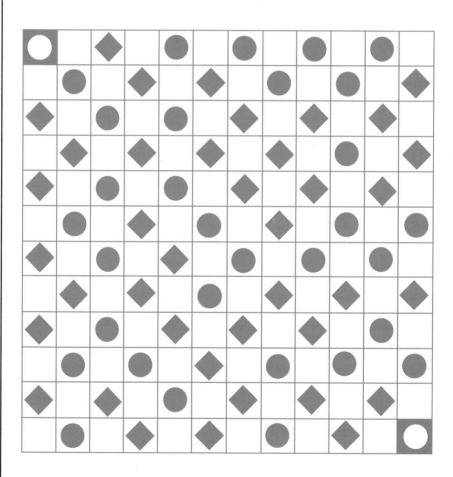

Answer on page 189.

Logidoku

The numbers 1 to 9 are to be placed once in every row, column, long diagonal, irregular shape, and 3 by 3 grid. From the numbers given, can you complete the puzzle?

9			4					
	5				6		8	
8			9					
				1				3
			7					
		4						
		2		6				5
							2	

Trivia on the Brain

No one fully understands how a human brain can tell the body how to pick up a glass of water. If we did, it would be a major achievement.

U.S. Tour Scramblegram

Four 11-letter words, all of which revolve around the same theme, have been jumbled. Unscramble the words, and write the answers in the accompanying space. Next, transfer the letters that are in the shaded boxes into the shaded keyword space, and unscramble the 9-letter word that goes with the theme. The theme for this puzzle is U.S. cities.

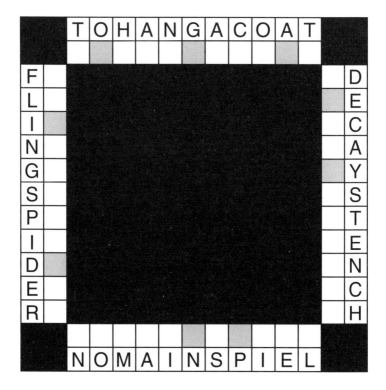

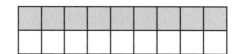

Answers on page 189.

1-2-3

Place the numbers 1, 2, or 3 in the circles below. The challenge is to have only these 3 numbers in each connected row and column—no number should repeat. Any combination is allowed.

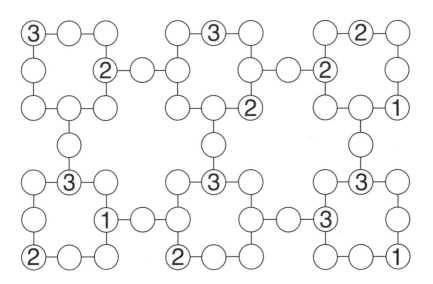

Mail Service

Across

1. Achieve through deception
8. Native Israeli
13. "Told you so"
14. Really dug
15. Chump
16. Smiling
17. _____ Conner,
    Miss USA 2006
18. Seemed likely
20. Tonto's horse
22. Wade opponent
23. Emergency med. procedure
24. Sings the praises of
26. Obligation
27. Business address, perhaps
31. Parliamentary procedures?
32. Hubbub
33. KITT or General Lee
34. New Deal monogram
35. Emulated a sous chef
39. Tree carvings
42. Malcolm Arnold's "Fantasy
    for Cello," for example
43. Fabrications
44. Best possible
46. Latin clarifier
47. Childlike attitude
48. Gives off, as light
49. Met at the door

Down

1. Partner of figures
2. Violinist Stern
3. Part of TNT
4. Attacks
5. Disparity
6. Tale-teller
7. "Terminator 2" costar
8. Noncom's nickname
9. Plugging away
10. Den denizen
11. Approach quickly
12. Bird in "B.C."
19. Polite refusal
21. Chinese ideal
25. Norwegian "ouch"
26. Putting down
27. Promoting peace
28. National anthem since 1980
29. Three make a turkey
30. Potential bait-taker
34. Bruce Lee's weapons
36. Doomsday cause, perhaps
37. Fill with happiness
38. Handed (out)
40. Experiment
41. Category of crystals
45. Casual Friday omission

Mondrianize It!

Inspired by the artwork of Belgian artist Piet Mondrian, these puzzles consist of stars and circles. Using the checkered pattern as a guide, draw in lines so that each star is in its own square and each circle in its own rectangle.

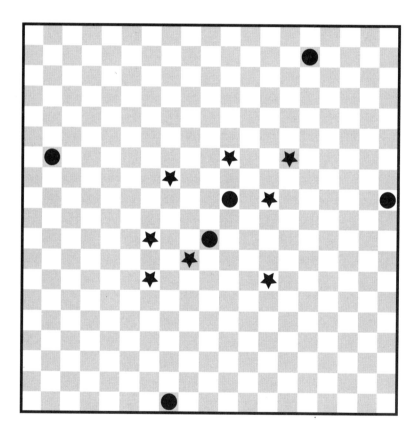

Answer on page 190.

Stack the Deck

This puzzle is actually 2 puzzles in 1! For the first puzzle, find a single, unbroken path from the outlined spade in the upper left corner to the outlined club in the lower right corner. You can only move diagonally, and you must alternate between spades and clubs as you move. For the second puzzle, start at the outlined heart in the upper right corner, and alternate between hearts and diamonds to find an unbroken path to the outlined diamond in the lower left corner.

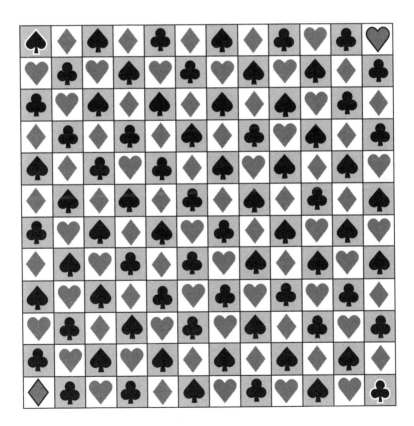

Perfect Score

Make 3 successful hits so that the sum of the numbers is 100. Double and triple scores do not apply. Numbers may be used more than once.

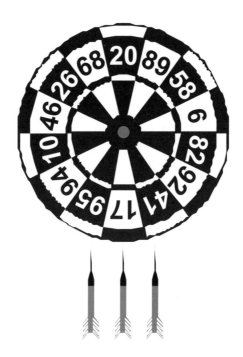

Trivia on the Brain

Research has shown that the newest cells in your brain can be taught more easily than the more mature cells.

Answer on page 190.

Digital Sudoku

LOGIC

Fill in the grid so that each row, column, and 2 by 3 block contains the numbers 1 through 6 exactly once. Numbers are in digital form, and some segments have already been filled in.

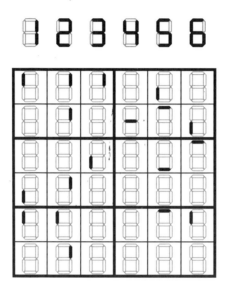

Liar's Logic!

ANALYSIS

LOGIC

Decipher the statements below using the following information to figure out who is lying and who is telling the truth. There are 2 truth-tellers, and 3 liars. Assume that each participant is feeling only one emotion.

A. I'm anxious, B is bored, and C is calm.

B. I'm bored, C is calm, and D is depressed.

C. I'm confident, D is delighted, and E is elated.

D. I'm delighted, E is elated, and A is angry.

E. I'm envious, A is anxious, and B is bored.

Who are the liars, and whose mood can't we be sure about, if any?

LANGUAGE

Five-Letter Anagrams

Fill in the blanks in each sentence below with five-letter words that are anagrams (rearrangements of the same letters) of one another.

1. Six A.M. is too ___ to run a ___ race.

2. The ___ disappeared from the stockroom without a ___.

3. The ___ set called for 3 ___ in the fence.

4. The nurse ___ for all his patients, so it shouldn't ___ you to go to the hospital.

5. You will ___ a traffic regulation if you don't ___ at the red light.

6. A ___ pair of sunglasses may cut down on the ___ from the sun.

Trivia on the Brain

The first cervical dorsal spinal nerve and dorsal root ganglia—which help bring sensory information into the brain and spinal cord—are missing in 50 percent of all people.

Answers on page 190.

Answers

Quic-Kross (page 6)

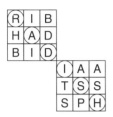

RADISH

Anagrams at Work (page 6)

general/enlarge

Crossed Words (page 7)

1-2-3 (page 8)

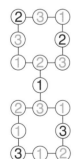

Odd One Out (page 9)

HE. The other words sound like parts of the human body.

L'adder (page 9)

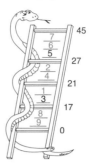

45
7
6
5
27
2
4
21
1
3
17
8
9
0

Perfect Score (page 10)

6 + 34 + 60 = 100

Sudoku (page 11)

2	3	8	1	9	7	6	4	5
4	9	5	2	6	3	7	1	8
1	7	6	5	4	8	3	2	9
8	2	7	6	1	5	9	3	4
5	1	4	3	8	9	2	6	7
9	6	3	4	7	2	8	5	1
6	4	9	8	2	1	5	7	3
7	5	2	9	3	4	1	8	6
3	8	1	7	5	6	4	9	2

Three of a Kind (page 11)

1. arm/ram; 2. dub/Bud; 3. nip/pin; 4. cat/act; 5. bad/dab

Marbles (page 12)

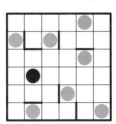

Answers

Hashi (page 13)

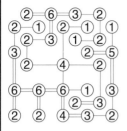

Cross Count (page 14)

¹s	⁸h	⁵e	14
⁷p	⁵e	⁵n	17
¹a	⁵n	⁴d	10
9	18	14	

Number Climber (page 15)

Job Jibes (pages 16–17)

Army Show (page 18)

	Title	Surname	Act
1	Private	Buckshot	juggling
2	Major	Bark	comedy
3	Colonel	Rattle	acting
4	Sergeant	Trumpet	piano

Contain Yourself (page 19)

ex(pen)sive, vau(devil)le, c(Handel)ier

You Can Count on This (page 19)

If the Lord had wanted us to use the metric system, there would have been ten apostles.

The Shading Game (page 20)

Word Columns (page 21)

As soon as you sit down to a cup of hot coffee, your boss will ask you to do something which will last until the coffee is cold.

Between the Lines (pages 22–23)

Mammoth, man, manacle;
rumpus, run, runaway;
manuscript, many, map;
riser, risk, risqué;
sister, sit, sitar

"A man sits as many risks as he runs."

Word Jigsaw (page 23)

```
    A R K
V A L U E
A L O N G
T E E
```

The Fruit Vendor's Cart
(page 24)

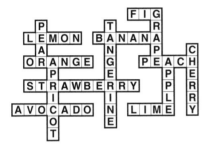

Fences (page 25)

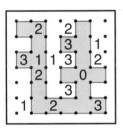

Word Ladder (page 25)

BLOND, bland, brand, BRAID

Honeycomb (page 26)

Code-doku (page 27)

HEMINGWAY

Odd One Out (page 27)

HEN. All the other words can be used as verbs.

Hashi (page 28)

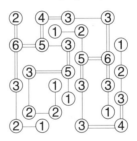

Flying High (page 29)

COANFL	F A L C O N
RIOBN	R O B I N
CAALINRD	C A R D I N A L
NAARYC	C A N A R Y
BIRDULEB	B L U E B I R D
WOCR	C R O W
EGLAE	E A G L E
WSROPRA	S P A R R O W
GASLIRNT	S T A R L I N G

F R E E   A S   A   B I R D

On the Slant (page 30)

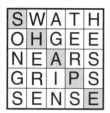

S	W	A	T	H
O	H	G	E	E
N	E	A	R	S
G	R	I	P	S
S	E	N	S	E

Diagonal word: SHAPE

A Puzzling Perspective
(page 31)

Graduations

Name Calling (page 32)

Cast in your lot among us, let us all have one purse.

A Beatles' Triple Sequence
(page 32)

P: All Things Must Pass

Number Crossword (page 33)

2	4	6	
3	4	5	6
1	2	4	8
	2	3	6

Acrostic Clues (pages 34–35)

A. Ralph Waldo Emerson; B. Russia; C. dynamite; D. washout; E. testifies; F. Sweden; G. hibernate; H. halibut; I. twitch

"What lies behind us and what lies before us are tiny matters compared to what lies within us."

Cone You Top This?
(pages 36–37)

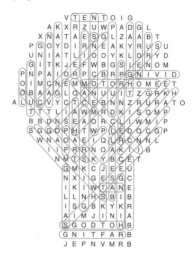

Vowel Play (pages 38–39)

Match-Up Twins (page 40)

The matching pairs are: 1 and 8, 2 and 9, 3 and 6, 4 and 7, 5 and 10.

Word of Mouth (page 41)

T	O	H	U	M
H	U	M	T	O
M	T	O	H	U
O	H	U	M	T
U	M	T	O	H

Hashi (page 42)

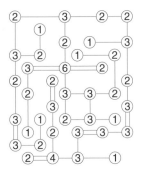

Elevator Words (page 43)

1. KNOW how; 2. how come;
3. come clean; 4. clean hands;
5. hands off; 6. off base; 7. base HIT

Missing Connections
(page 44)

Geometric Cube Construction (page 45)

Cube C can be made from the unfolded sample.

Star Power (page 46)

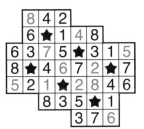

Kakuro (page 47)

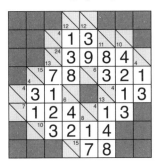

Cross Count (page 48)

^{9}r	^{6}o	^{7}p	^{5}e	27
^{1}a	^{2}b	^{3}l	^{5}e	11
^{6}f	^{6}o	^{1}a	^{3}l	16
^{2}t	^{5}e	^{5}n	^{1}s	13
18	19	16	14	

Anagram Pickup (page 49)

insulted/unlisted

Letters to Numbers (page 49)

8	1	6
3	5	7
4	9	2

Quic-Kross (page 50)

(A)	R	G	U	E
I	(N)	L	E	T
A	F	(T)	E	R
A	H	E	(A)	D
L	A	T	E	(R)

(C)	S	S	C	P
R	(T)	T	O	A
I	O	(I)	U	S
S	N	N	(C)	T
P	E	T	H	(A)

ANTARCTICA

Cube Count (page 51)

There are 57 cubes.

Crossing Caution

(pages 52–53)

C	A	L	F		R	A	V	I		R	A	B	B	I
A	B	E	L		I	R	A	N		U	N	L	I	T
T	U	N	A		G	I	M	P		S	I	E	N	A
S	T	O	P	T	H	E	P	R	E	S	S	E	S
		J	U	T	S		I	V	I	E	D	
C	A	M	A	R	O		A	V	I	A		W	P	A
A	M	O	C	O		H	E	A	T		S	H	O	R
L	O	O	K	W	H	O	S	T	A	L	K	I	N	G
I	N	N	S		A	L	O	E		O	U	T	D	O
F	G	S		P	R	E	P		M	O	L	E	S	T
	H	A	I	T	I		T	A	S	K	
	L	I	S	T	E	N	T	O	R	E	A	S	O	N
S	O	N	A	R		O	H	N	O		W	A	K	E
S	T	E	N	O		N	A	T	O		A	T	R	A
S	T	R	A	W		E	T	O	N		Y	E	A	R

Word Jigsaw (page 54)

Talk Show (page 55)

	Name	Surname	Topic
1	Jackie	Bore	book
2	Bruce	Ponds	baseball
3	Hal	Rawlings	movie
4	Gary	Wells	politics

Cluster (page 56)

Dubious Dictionary (page 57)

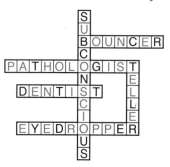

Word Columns (page 58)

If a trio of doctors who specialized in tonsillectomies formed a singing group with no instruments they could call themselves "Ahhh Capella."

Calcu-doku (page 59)

2	5	1	3	4
4	3	5	2	1
3	2	4	1	5
1	4	3	5	2
5	1	2	4	3

Circle Takes the Square
(page 60)

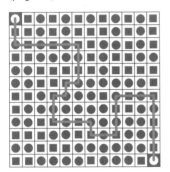

Jewelry Scramblegram
(page 63)

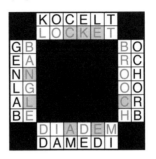

Card Shark (page 61)

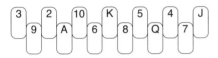

Sudoku (page 64)

5	1	9	8	7	4	3	2	6
3	4	2	9	1	6	7	8	5
7	6	8	3	2	5	1	9	4
8	9	1	6	5	2	4	3	7
6	2	3	4	9	7	8	5	1
4	5	7	1	3	8	9	6	2
2	3	4	7	6	9	5	1	8
1	8	5	2	4	3	6	7	9
9	7	6	5	8	1	2	4	3

Marbles (page 62)

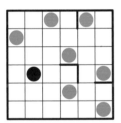

Take Me Out to the Ball Game (page 62)

```
  9648 BASE
  9622 BALL
+16784 GAMES
———————————
 36054 YANKS
```
A=6, B=9, E=8, G=1, K=5, L=2,
M=7, N=0, S=4, Y=3

L'adder (page 65)

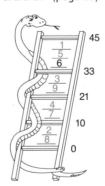

177

Number Challenge
(pages 66–67)

2	1	■	6	1
2	3	4	5	6
■	7	7	5	■
7	9	3	5	1
7	5	■	6	5

Say What? (page 67)

"To invent, you need a good imagination and a pile of junk."

1-2-3 (page 68)

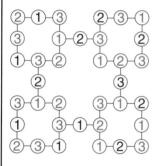

Name Search (page 69)

ROB wins. His name appears 13 times. BOB, even though it can be spelled forward and backward, appears only 12 times. The hidden word is ORB.

Fitting Words (page 70)

S	I	L	A	S
P	O	I	S	E
A	W	A	I	T
S	A	R	A	H

Odd-Even Logidoku
(page 71)

8	2	9	3	5	1	6	7	4
3	5	6	4	9	7	1	8	2
1	4	7	6	8	2	3	9	5
4	7	3	9	2	6	5	1	8
9	6	2	5	1	8	7	4	3
5	1	8	7	4	3	2	6	9
7	8	5	2	6	9	4	3	1
6	9	4	1	3	5	8	2	7
2	3	1	8	7	4	9	5	6

Warning: Curves Ahead
(page 72)

ABCD (page 73)

A	B	A	B	A	D
D	C	B	A	D	B
C	B	C	B	C	D
A	C	A	D	A	B
C	B	C	B	D	C
D	A	D	A	B	D

Perfect Score (page 74)

11 + 35 + 54 = 100

Star Power (page 75)

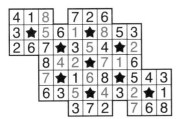

Spell Math! (page 75)

Two + eighteen = twenty

Card Shark (page 76)

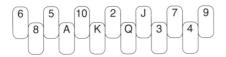

Hashi (page 77)

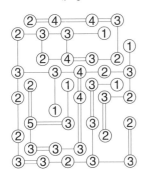

Wonders Down Under
(pages 78–79)

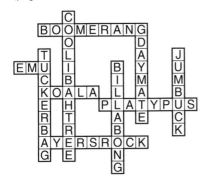

Fashionable Scramblegram (page 80)

Identity Parade (page 81)

A   B   C   D

Musicians Letterbox
(page 82)

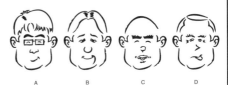

1	2	3	4	5	6	7	8	9	10	11	12	13
H	J	Z	V	T	K	L	Q	A	G	B	N	D

14	15	16	17	18	19	20	21	22	23	24	25	26
W	E	R	O	X	Y	M	U	S	I	C	F	P

Fitting Words (page 83)

B	A	T	H	E
A	L	I	E	N
N	O	M	A	D
K	E	E	P	S

What's the Time? (page 83)

It is 23 minutes before noon.
23 minutes less than 12:00 noon
is 11:37, and 28 minutes less than
11:37 is 11:09. 69 minutes (3 times
23) after 10 A.M. is 11:09.

179

Answers

Cube Count (page 84)

There are 79 cubes.

Battle Boats (page 85)

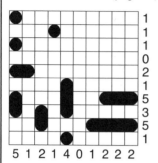

1
1
1
0
2
1
5
3
5
1

5 1 2 1 4 0 1 2 2 2

Hitori (page 86)

1	2	4	3	7	5	1	8
1	5	3	8	5	1	6	4
4	1	5	3	2	3	6	6
3	6	2	5	4	8	7	1
7	5	1	7	8	2	4	3
6	3	5	2	5	4	7	7
2	4	8	8	6	4	1	5
5	2	6	1	6	7	3	6

Get It Straight (page 87)

Word Columns (page 88)

No matter how grouchy you're feeling,/You'll find a smile more or less healing./It grows in a wreath/ All around the front teeth—/Thus preserving the face from congealing.

Masyu (page 89)

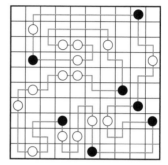

Odd One Out (page 90)

YOU'LL is the odd one out. The others form words when the apostrophe is removed.

L'adder (page 90)

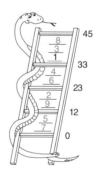

45
$\frac{8}{3}$
$\frac{1}{1}$
33
$\frac{4}{6}$
23
$\frac{2}{9}$
12
$\frac{5}{7}$
0

Hobby Horse (page 91)

A. INSPIRATION is not a pleasant hobby; B. photography; C. gardening; D. woodcarving

Stick Figures

(page 92)

Figure B appeared twice.

Rhyme Time (page 92)

1. wise guys; 2. dark park; 3. aching raking; 4. treason reason; 5. Esau's seesaws

Hamster Treadmill (page 93)

Device A is correct.

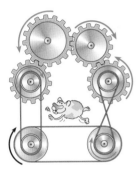

Hashi (page 94)

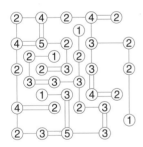

Kakuro (page 95)

		9	12				3	12	6
17	8	9	6			8	1	2
6	1	2	3	18	1	2	4
3	1	2	24	8	7	9
6	1	2	3	13
24	8	7	9	16	14
13	1	9	3	4	1	3	9
11	1	3	7	24	7	9	8
7	2	5	3	2	1

Clapboard (pages 96–97)

¹C	²L	³I	⁴N	⁵G	⁶A	⁷B	⁸S	⁹I	¹⁰G	¹¹N	¹²E	¹³D
¹⁴E	E	R	I	¹⁵E	R	E	¹⁶A	D	O	O	N	E
¹⁷E	N	¹⁸A	B	L	I	¹⁹N	G	A	R	D	E	N
²⁰S	I	B	²¹S	L	E	²²D	I	²³S	E	²⁴E	²⁵M	S
²⁶U	²⁷N	I	T	²⁸E	S	I	F	T	E	²⁹R	³⁰Y	³¹E
³²S	E	D	E	R	³³A	³⁴P	³⁵T	³⁶A	R	I	E	L
³⁷T	³⁸E	³⁹E	M	U	⁴⁰I	R	⁴¹I	G	U	⁴²S	⁴³T	⁴⁴S
⁴⁵A	⁴⁶R	⁴⁷N	E	E	⁴⁸D	U	D	⁴⁹S	L	E	E	T
⁵⁰I	O	T	⁵¹A	⁵²S	A	⁵³D	⁵⁴E	T	E	N	⁵⁵T	E
⁵⁶N	⁵⁷E	R	D	⁵⁸I	D	⁵⁹E	⁶⁰W	⁶¹A	⁶²R	O	O	T
⁶³U	⁶⁴K	E	R	⁶⁵N	A	V	E	⁶⁶L	⁶⁷U	⁶⁸R	⁶⁹E	⁷⁰S
⁷¹D	⁷²E	E	A	⁷³C	H	E	⁷⁴R	A	⁷⁵D	E	D	E
⁷⁶E	⁷⁷S	S	T	E	L	L	⁷⁸A	G	E	N	D	A

Magic Square (page 98)

8	2	10	4	6
4	6	8	2	10
2	10	4	6	8
6	8	2	10	4
10	4	6	8	2

Flip the Cards (page 99)

The answer is D. You don't need to make sure that all 8 cards have an F on the reverse, just that all F cards have a number on the reverse.

Name That Name (page 100)

First Name	Surname	Profession
Tony	Sparrow	Entertainer
Samuel	Painter	Carpenter
Frank	Cook	Chauffeur
Samantha	Kitchen	Tailor
Alan	Wood	Baker
Annette	Driver	Cook
Julia	Singer	Ornithologist

Word Ladder (page 100)

Answers may vary.
SLED, sued, sues, hues, hugs, huge, LUGE

Answers

Digital Sudoku (page 101)

5	3	6	8	2	4
2	4	8	5	3	6
8	6	4	3	5	2
3	5	2	4	6	8
6	8	5	2	4	3
4	2	3	6	8	5

Crypto-Logic (page 101)

GENIUS. If A is 8 then B is 2, and 2I is therefore 2, making I worth 1. E is 4, and so G is 6. R is worth 10, and so U is 5, and N is 9. 9 - 2 = S, which is therefore 7.

Cross-Math (page 102)

7	-	1	÷	3	=	2
+		+		×		
8	×	2	+	4	=	20
÷		+		-		
5	+	9	+	6	=	20
=		=		=		
3		12		6		

Grid Fill (page 103)

B	L	I	N	D	S
O	V	E	R	L	Y
A	T	T	I	R	E
H	O	U	R	L	Y
F	I	N	I	T	E
L	A	P	S	E	D
G	A	R	A	G	E

Fitting Words (page 104)

P	S	H	A	W
A	W	A	R	E
R	A	V	E	N
K	N	E	A	D

Maggie's List (page 105)

Choice C is correct. The numbers in question are all multiples of 9. The number 891 is the only choice of the four options that is also a multiple of 9.

Circular Memory (page 106)

D is the circle arrangement that appeared twice on page 105.

Party Time (page 106)

Several historical figures were invited to a party. Einstein said it would be relatively easy to attend. Schubert said he'd come, but there was something he had to finish first. Dr. Jekyll was of two minds...

Star Power (page 107)

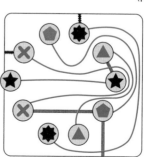

Uncrossed Paths (page 108)

Hashi (page 109)

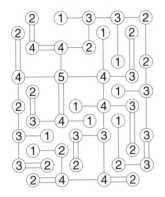

Perfect Score (page 110)

$17 + 25 + 58 = 100$

Word Columns (page 111)

"It's snowing still," said Eeyore gloomily. "So it is." "And freezing." "Is it?" "Yes," said Eeyore. "However," he said, brightening up a little, "we haven't had an earthquake lately."

—A.A. Milne

Word Ladder (page 112)

STRAP, straw, strew, screw, scraw, scram, scrum, serum, STRUM

Twenty-four Jumble
(page 112)

$4 - 2 \times 9 + 6 = 24$

Round and Round (page 114)

Earth, Pizza, Ship's wheel, Soccer ball, Stopwatch

Marbles (page 115)

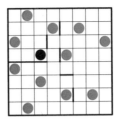

Name Calling (page 116)

Don't rejoice at your enemy's fall, but don't rush to pick him up either.

Buried Nuts (page 117)

	Tree	Location	No. Nuts
1	beech	river	15
2	cedar	garden	10
3	dogwood	lake	8
4	elm	fence	7
5	ash	park	5
6	fir	wood	12

Missing Connections
(page 118)

Answers

You Are Here (page 119)

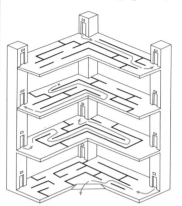

Mondrianize It! (page 123)

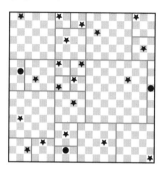

Traffic Light (pages 120–121)

A	T	L	A	W	■	P	I	S	A	■	M	A	P	S
B	O	O	L	A	■	A	L	E	C	■	E	R	O	O
B	B	A	L	L	■	P	E	E	R	■	A	K	I	N
R	E	D	S	K	Y	A	T	M	O	R	N	I	N	G
■	■	■	W	I	T	S	■	■	S	A	I	N	T	S
L	E	G	E	N	D	■	B	E	T	T	E	■	■	■
A	D	U	L	T	■	A	U	D	I	■	■	F	B	I
Y	E	L	L	O	W	B	R	I	C	K	R	O	A	D
S	N	L	■	■	C	U	B	E	■	A	A	N	D	E
■	■	■	T	U	F	T	S	■	P	R	I	Z	E	D
A	G	A	S	S	I	■	■	P	E	E	N	■	■	■
G	R	E	E	N	E	G	G	S	A	N	D	H	A	M
L	E	S	T	■	L	O	L	A	■	I	R	A	T	E
O	T	I	S	■	D	U	E	L	■	N	O	N	O	S
W	A	R	E	■	S	T	E	M	■	A	P	S	E	S

Circular Reasoning (page 124)

Odd-Even Logidoku
(page 122)

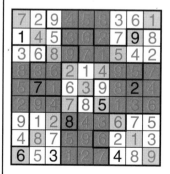

ABCD (page 125)

D	C	B	A	B	A	D	B	C
A	B	A	C	A	B	A	C	B
D	C	D	A	C	D	C	D	C
C	B	A	B	D	A	B	C	D
A	C	B	A	C	B	A	B	C
D	B	C	B	A	C	B	D	B

Quic-Kross (page 126)

(A)	R	M	E	D
A	(B)	I	D	E
B	A	(S)	T	E
S	H	O	(O)	T
J	E	W	E	(L)

(U)	A	B	B	O
N	(T)	R	R	R
I	O	(I)	O	I
O	N	N	(O)	O
N	E	G	D	(N)

ABSOLUTION

Word Paths (page 127)

1. Waste not, want not; 2. Look before you leap; 3. Practice what you preach; 4. A stitch in time saves nine

Red, White, Blue, and Green (pages 128–129)

G	W	B	W	G	B	R	R
B	R	G	G	W	R	W	B
W	G	B	R	R	B	G	W
R	B	W	B	G	G	W	R
G	B	R	G	W	R	B	W
W	G	R	R	B	W	B	G
R	W	G	W	B	G	R	B
B	R	W	B	R	W	G	G

Hitori (page 130)

4	4	1	8	5	2	7	5
7	5	3	2	6	3	1	4
8	4	3	7	5	5	6	1
4	6	3	5	4	8	4	2
5	3	8	8	7	1	2	4
8	1	5	3	5	7	2	6
3	5	7	4	1	6	8	5
6	8	4	8	2	2	5	1

Grid Fill (page 131)

S	A	L	U	T	E
S	T	R	A	N	D
A	R	C	H	E	S
I	N	S	I	D	E
T	A	L	O	N	S
S	O	D	I	U	M
C	L	O	S	E	T

Word-a-Maze: Avian Home (pages 132–133)

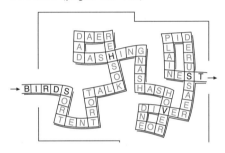

Code-doku (page 134)

A	U	L	K	C	P	B	E	R
E	K	R	L	B	A	C	P	U
C	B	P	R	E	U	A	L	K
K	P	U	E	A	B	R	C	L
L	E	B	U	R	C	P	K	A
R	A	C	P	L	K	E	U	B
U	R	A	C	P	L	K	B	E
P	L	E	B	K	R	U	A	C
B	C	K	A	U	E	L	R	P

PEARL BUCK

Wacky Wordy (page 134)

Father-in-law (DAD inside of JUDGE)

185

Hashi (page 135)

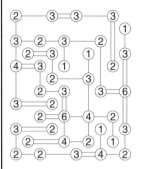

1-2-3 (page 136)

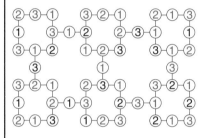

Kakuro (page 137)

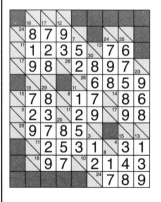

Word Jigsaw (page 138)

Tamagram (page 138)

ITALIC END = IDENTICAL

Vex-a-Gon (page 139)

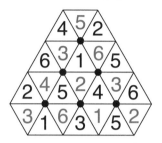

The Yellow-Brick Road
(page 140)

C. If you ask the truth-teller, he will tell you truthfully that the liar will tell you that he would lie and tell you to take the wrong road. If you ask the liar, he will lie and tell you that the truth-teller will lie and tell you that he, the liar, will tell the truth, giving the right road. It is impossible to know which road to take.

Arrow Web (page 141)

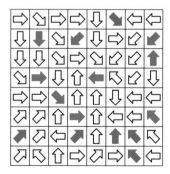

Togs (pages 142–143)

Cluster (page 146)

Tessellated Floor (page 144)

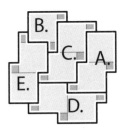

Marbles (page 147)

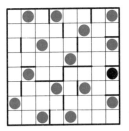

Add It Up (page 145)

Answers may vary.

7	5	8	3	2	2	6	5	1	8	**47**
1	2	5	3	2	1	6	5	8	9	**42**
7	3	4	2	1	6	5	8	1	2	**39**
1	6	2	3	8	1	7	4	9	5	**46**
9	1	4	3	1	5	1	2	3	9	**38**
5	5	9	1	6	5	4	6	5	7	**53**
8	8	6	9	4	6	2	8	9	2	**62**
6	2	1	3	7	4	7	7	1	8	**46**
7	7	2	5	3	8	3	2	3	7	**47**
4	3	8	4	2	4	1	4	5	9	**44**
55	**42**	**49**	**36**	**36**	**42**	**42**	**51**	**45**	**66**	**43**

63

Wacky Wordy (page 147)

A little goes a long way

Red, White, Blue, and Green (pages 148–149)

```
G G R W R B W B
B W G R W B R G
G G W B R W R B
W B B R G R G W
B W R G B W G R
R R B W W G B G
R R W G B G B W
W B G B G R W R
```

Get It Straight (page 150)

Word Columns (page 151)

"Protect me from knowing what I don't need to know. Protect me from even knowing that there are things to know that I don't know. Protect me from knowing that I decided not to know about the things that I decided not to know about. Amen."

—Douglas Adams

Hashi (page 152)

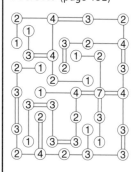

Cross Sums (page 153)

				1453				
			428	465	383			
		72	125	177	110	54		
	8	7	54	53	42	6	2	
	3	11	28	9	4			
		12	5	1				
			10					

Stopping for Directions (page 154)

Row B is correct.

Strings Attached (page 155)

SCARLET CAD = CAT'S CRADLE; SOPHIE FLING = FISHING POLE; TRAINEE TOM = MARIONETTE; ANCIENT TREKS = TENNIS RACKET; TOE BOIL = BOLO TIE; BLIMP LUNE = PLUMB LINE; DAMN LION = MANDOLIN

Number Crossword (page 156)

5	3		8	7
2	2	2	2	2
	5	3	1	
1	9	4	2	2
3	1		8	3

Star Power (page 157)

Codeword (page 158)

```
D E F Y ■ E L I T I S T S
O   L   D   U   E   Q   T
U R A N I U M ■ M A U V E
B   I   S   M   P   E   R
L A R G O ■ O V E R A W E
E   ■ B   X   R   L   O
J E S T E R ■ B A S S E T
O   H   D   B   T   ■ Y
I T E M I Z E ■ U S U R P
N   I   E   V   R   N   I
T O K E N ■ E L E G I A C
E   H   C   L   S   T   A
D I S P E N S E ■ S E L L
```

1	2	3	4	5	6	7	8	9	10	11	12	13
A	Y	R	U	F	D	I	G	S	L	C	O	M

14	15	16	17	18	19	20	21	22	23	24	25	26
P	B	X	J	Q	K	W	Z	H	N	T	V	E

No Bones About It (page 159)

1. d) rhomboid; 2. c) pointal;
3. b) paella; 4. c) perpendicular;
5. d) porkal; 6. a) vertical;
7. d) pimpal; 8. b) capital

Diamond in the Rough
(page 160)

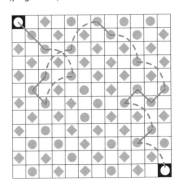

Logidoku (page 161)

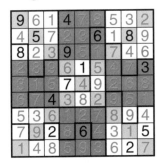

U.S. Tour Scramblegram
(page 162)

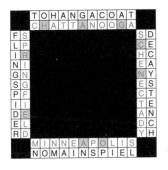

1-2-3 (page 163)

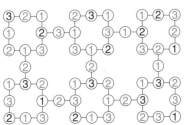

Mail Service (pages 164–165)

F	I	N	A	G	L	E		S	A	B	R	A
A	S	I	S	A	I	D		A	T	E	U	P
C	A	T	S	P	A	W		R	I	A	N	T
T	A	R	A		R	A	N	G	T	R	U	E
S	C	O	U	T		R	O	E		C	P	R
		L	A	U	D	S		D	U	T	Y	
P	O	S	T	O	F	F	I	C	E	B	O	X
A	C	T	S		F	U	R	O	R			
C	A	R		F	D	R		D	I	C	E	D
I	N	I	T	I	A	L	S		S	O	L	O
F	A	K	E	S		O	P	T	I	M	A	L
I	D	E	S	T		N	A	I	V	E	T	E
C	A	S	T	S		G	R	E	E	T	E	D

Digital Sudoku (page 169)

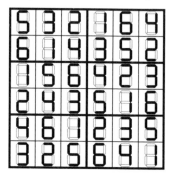

Mondrianize It! (page 166)

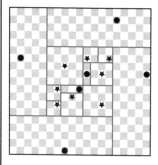

Stack the Deck (page 167)

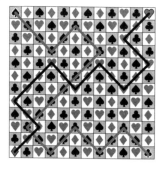

Perfect Score (page 168)

6 + 26 + 68 = 100

Liar's Logic! (page 169)

The liars are A, B, and E. If somebody agrees with A on a subject, then A may be a truth-teller. But if 2 or more people are in agreement with A over any subject (even 2 different points of agreement), then A cannot be a truth-teller, as there are only 2 of them. The sole combination that works, given this arrangement, is for C and D to be the truth-tellers. We cannot be sure about B's mood.

Five-Letter Anagrams (page 170)

1. early/relay; 2. crate/trace;
3. stage/gates; 4. cares/scare;
5. break/brake; 6. large/glare

Index

Index